6-12-80

For more than twenty-five years, George McManus has been a highly esteemed reporter and commentator on the steel industry. His continual contact with various labor and business leaders has given him a first-hand education in the nation's economic organization. In this defense of prosperity, he boldly confronts the economic problems facing us today, examines our present economic structure, and sets forth the conditions for growth.

The author's case for capitalism is expressed here with unusual concern for the well-being and prosperity of *every* American. Both conservative and liberal arguments are accounted for in the author's plain statement of faith in the free enterprise system which has created unparalleled wealth, broadly distributed.

In his analysis, which is buttressed by a review of recent economic history, he carefully considers the problems of income redistribution and the needs of business—and argues that the American nation is in trouble. Excessive taxation is dangerously reducing the supply of capital, damping the creative drive of individuals, and preventing growth and prosperity. He points out that the vast sums already being transferred from the affluent to the less affluent should serve, if properly handled, to eliminate poverty. And to those who oppose tax reductions on inflationary grounds, he demonstrates that modern inflation is not caused by too much demand and has persisted in good times and bad. The book concludes with proposals for dealing with inflation's real causes and a challenge to conventional antidotes.

In Defense of Prosperity

A Commonsense Case for Capitalism

George J. McManus

CHILTON BOOK COMPANY /RADNOR, PENNSYLVANIA

1 2 3 4 5 6 7 8 9 0   8 7 6 5 4 3 2 1 0 9

Contents

Contents

In Defense of Prosperity

Chapter 1

THE PRIVATE SECTOR AND THE PUBLIC GOOD

Whille vacationing at the Jersey shore, my wife and I wandered down to a boat basin. Moored at slips were a number of cabin cruisers, each about forty feet long and broad beamed. There were elaborate rigs for fishing. We asked a man who looked as though he might know how much a boat like that would cost. He said $250,000. Someone else said the boat used ninety gallons of fuel an hour. We nodded our heads and walked away.

In the distance was a large marina. Jammed in were probably a hundred or more boats of various sizes. They weren't all luxury liners, but most were substantial looking. We marveled at the wealth that had to go into all this. To be able to spend a quarter of a million dollars was completely outside of our experience and beyond our means.

A LAND OF WEALTH

It is not just that some people are very rich; a great many people seem to possess extreme wealth. In Pittsburgh, Pennsylvania, there are days when every other car seems to be a

$20,000 Mercedes. In Ocean City, Maryland, you drive past rows of new condominiums. The signs say: "One and two bedrooms, $60,000 and up." In Youngstown, Ohio, there are houses that look as if they sell for more than $200,000.

You wouldn't be surprised if a few amenities went with the job of president of the United States or chief executive of United States Steel. But when you drive past the $200,000 homes, you see names like C. T. Lindquist or F. X. Crowley. Two thoughts emerge from this. One is that America must be a great place in order to have so many wealthy people. It is a reassuring tribute that you don't have to be a captain of industry to lead the good life in the U. S. A. On second thought, however, you find it difficult to believe all these anonymous individuals deserve to be so wealthy on the basis of their contributions. This difficulty is doubtless increased if you happen to be among the 25 million persons officially classed in 1976 as poverty stricken.

The question arises: Why should some people live in great luxury while others are impoverished? Why shouldn't government take some of the excess wealth and distribute it among the poor people.

The standard answer has been that the American system of uneven rewards produces more good things for everyone than systems that commandeer all output and distribute it according to needs. A cornerstone of the private enterprise is the notion that an individual should keep a large portion of the wealth he creates. This provides an incentive for people to work hard. The more productive the individual is, the more the whole society benefits, including those at the bottom.

Closely related to this notion is one theory of capital formation. Unequal income distribution is seen as a mechanism for channeling a portion of what is produced back into machines to turn out future goods. Some people are given more than they need to survive, even on a grand scale.

In the form of savings or retained company earnings or stock purchases, the leftover portion goes into renewing and expanding the productive system.

Some people today believe that the forces and funds that flow from inequality are being diminished to a critical extent by the downward transfer of income, a transfer they see as encouraging sloth among those on the receiving end. Income transfer is discouraging innovation and effort, they say. Income transfer is also seen as taking badly needed capital from individuals and corporations, the result starvation of the productive system as income is channeled into consumption.

The argument continues that redistribution has reached the point of diminishing returns. Government is taking a larger share of a shrinking pie, and by choking off growth, government's incursion will eventually leave less income to be transferred. At the same time, the lack of private growth will create pressure for more social spending and a still larger share of output. Those at the bottom will suffer most, partly because the net transfer will be reduced, but more importantly because lack of growth will restrict the ability of the private system to employ people and elevate their living standards.

The remedy proposed is a tax reduction that would leave a larger share of income in the private sector and reduce the share being taken by government. A number of the specific proposals would have the effect of increasing the income shares of affluent individuals while reducing the share transferred to poor people. Stated in this manner, the proposals sound inhumane and immoral, but as will be discussed, there are good reasons for believing that the maximum rise in income levels of the poor can be achieved through a reduction in the income share transferred to the poor.

These general ideas are not new. For the past forty years, business people have been warning of a trend toward socialism (government control of income and output). A country becomes more socialistic as government's share of income increases. If this view is accepted, the warnings of business are becoming more valid, more specific, and more emphatic. Just before the Franklin D. Roosevelt era, government's share of Gross National Product was about 10 percent. Today, it is over 30 percent.

THE CHALLENGE TO FREE MARKET PRINCIPLES

While the principles of the free market are being reaffirmed, these principles are also being challenged by many educators, politicians, leaders of minority organizations, and others. The achievement of greater equality is given a high priority by one leading economist. "There is no excuse for inhumane penalties for losers. Whether or not gladiatorial contests were 'fair,' it was barbaric to feed the losers to the lions," said Arthur Okun of Brookings Institution.[1]

Okun and others contended a greater share of income should be transferred to "losers" in the U. S. system. The need was for more redistribution, not less. If there were some undesirable side effects, these were less important than the objective of a more just division of income. Until recently, this seemed to be the prevailing view, certainly in the sense of governing the course of events. The assumption was that politicians were responding to the needs and wants of most people.

Meanwhile, support for the old values was pretty much private and out of contact with public doings. In occupational meetings, businessmen told other businessmen the country was going to the dogs. The picture was one of a few old die-hards resisting progress. In 1978, however, support for the old ways surfaced, as will be detailed later in this chapter.

It turned out that very large numbers of people wanted the old ways preserved. Sensing the popular mood, politicians added their voices to the call for lower taxes and less income transfer.

Now under way is a "Great Debate" on the direction of the nation. The first skirmish, involving 1978 tax legislation, left both sides dissatisfied. It may, however, have marked a turning point. In the face of presidential opposition and in a Democratic Congress, conservative forces were able to secure a tax cut specifically benefiting capitalists.

At stake in all this is the kind of system the United States is to have. It is a statistical fact that the country has been moving toward socialism. Government's share of income has gone from one tenth to one third. If the trend of the last forty years continues, we will cease to be a nation in which people are rewarded or punished primarily by the workings of the free market.

A change from capitalism to socialism is not to be made lightly. It hasn't been shown that any other system is as effective as American capitalism in creating wealth. Despite complaints and agitation, it hasn't really been shown that any other system does as good a job of providing desirable social and economic good to people.

THE DRIVE FOR CAPITAL SUPPLY

The pressure to halt the current course of events is a reaction to the great increase in social spending, which now accounts for about half of all government outlays. It's argued that the enlargement of government can't continue without adverse effects to the private sector.

"There is a government sector which has been growing faster than the economy which supports it," said Reginald

Jones, chairman of General Electric Company. The son of a British steelworker, Jones has become leader of what might be called the capital formation movement. Asserting that "economies grow by setting aside part of their output and putting this into plants that will make people more productive," Jones charges that the American economy has been consuming its seed corn.

Initially, the drive to hold down taxes and income transfer was primarily a business concern and was debated within fairly narrow confines. In 1973 and 1974 there were shortages of many materials, helping produce the runaway inflation of those two years. It also provided evidence of a shortage of capital. There was relatively high unemployment during the two-year boom. The problem was not just an imbalance of supply and demand; there was an imbalance of men and machines. Businessmen said the shortages and the imbalance resulted from an inadequate supply of capital.

By 1975 business had marshaled arguments for tax measures to relieve the capital squeeze. In speeches and in congressional testimony, it was pointed out that U. S. productivity had been lagging in relation to the gains of other nations. The lag was related to the fact that in other countries larger shares of output were being put into capital programs.

But in the United States capital spending had not kept up with past needs, and enormous capital requirements lay ahead. Studies by the New York Stock Exchange, the U. S. Department of Commerce, and General Electric Company all pointed to a long-term future capital deficiency. "Under present tax policies, the capital requirements of nonfinancial corporations over the years immediately ahead will exceed available funds by $52 billion a year," said John deButts, chairman of American Telephone & Telegraph.

Inflation was adding to the problem. General Electric estimated higher prices would add 30 percent to capital needs over the next ten years or so. In addition, inflation was producing an overstatement of business profits and taxes. Corporations had nominal earnings of $65 billion in 1974, said William Simon. Adjusted for inflation, he said, true earnings were only $20 billion, and the effective tax role was 69 percent.

With inflation and high tax rates, businessmen contended, government was taxing away capital. The remedies proposed by business involved direct taxation: depreciation rules should be liberalized; the investment credit should be increased; the corporate tax rate should be reduced. A key point in the business pitch is that these tax reductions should be matched by curtailed government spending. It will do no good if government cuts taxes while federal deficits subtract the same amount from the capital pool.

The need for a larger capital supply was contested in 1975 congressional testimony by Joseph A. Pechman of Brookings Institution. Capital requirements could be met "without destroying the tax structure," said Pechman. He advised against proposals that "would reduce the taxes of corporations and high-income people when there is a public demand to remove tax preferences for investment income."

AFL-CIO President George Meany was more specific in his comments on the business tax package. "That's the old, discredited, trickle-down doctrine of the 1890s and 1920s," Meany told Congress in 1975. "Give those at the bottom less; squeeze those in the middle even more; give those at the top—especially the corporations—more tax shelters."

In rebuttal, companies argued that personal enrichment of business executives was an incidental side effect of tax relief, and was far overshadowed by the importance of providing more capital. "Businessmen are the visible and immediate beneficiaries of capitalism," said J. C. Beigler, senior partner of Price, Waterhouse & Co. "The income generated by capital investment goes largely to workers in the form of higher wages or to consumers in the form of better products for less money."

The relation between capital and jobs was stressed. "The most immediate need is to create jobs," said former Secretary Simon in 1976. "Between now and 1985, the labor force will expand by roughly fifteen million persons. In addition, there are at least three or four million unemployed persons in the labor force today [7.4 million were jobless in late 1976]. By comparison with the eighteen to nineteen million jobs that will thus be needed in the coming decade, our economy created thirteen to fifteen million jobs in the past decade."

All of which convinced few people in Washington. The initial business pitch—in 1975—was unfortunately timed. With the economy depressed and plants idle, there was no capital shortage. Companies were pulling back and holding down. There were a few minor gains that year, but business made little real progress in efforts to provide more capital. "The capital crusade of the Administration and much of the business community flopped," wrote Edwin Dale in the *New York Times* after the 1975 tax debate.

Business continued to plug away, but pressures for greater redistribution were mounting. The case against inequality of income distribution was set forth in impressive terms by Harvard Professor John Rawls. In *A Theory of Justice,* (Harvard University Press, 1971) Rawls held that such inequality was tolerable only if it benefited all income levels, including the lowest. Arthur Okun was among those critical of the gap between affluence and poverty. "The top 1 percent of families (those with roughly $50,000 and above) have as much after-tax income as nearly all the families in the bottom 20 percent," wrote Okun. This was a "terrible" situation.[2]

Groups like the National Welfare Rights Organization demanded greater redistribution as a matter of right, not charity. The sensitivity of political people to the demands and arguments was brought out in 1978 when a reduction in the capital gains tax was proposed. President Carter was outraged, calling this a boon to millionaires.

The sheer momentum of government spending made control difficult. Federal outlays went from $269 billion in fiscal year 1974 to $401 billion in 1977 and to an estimated $500 billion in 1979. Inflation was making for automatic increases in tax rates. Economic slack was making it difficult to prove there was a capital shortage and, with high unemployment, easy to show a need for more government spending.

Finally, tax relief for business faced a certain amount of automatic hostility. Big business was already making obscene profits, in the eyes of such observers as newspeople and public officials. Monopolies, payoffs, and other evil things were used to gouge the little people and thwart economic processes, they felt. It is a curiosity of our times that people in the media and government have profited from our system, yet they downgrade the nation's producers. This type of fallacious thinking has contributed to Britain's trouble, said Alan A. Walters, a University of London professor, who referred to the "amalgam of academic and bureaucrat and politician and their contempt for the businessman. If he behaves . . . then he may be allowed to continue his unsavory and demeaning pursuit."[3] It is not until a plant shutdown idles 5,000 in Youngstown, Ohio, that people realize a corporation is more than a few well-heeled executives. The steel shutdowns of 1977 showed that the well-being of communities and individuals is tied to the health of business.

THE TAX REBELLION

Going into 1978, it appeared the tide was running against business and others who favored a reversal of the tax and spending trends. The Carter tax package did contain some reduction for business, but cuts in individual income taxes were shaped so the "progressivity of the tax system will be increased."

Later in the year, however, there was a dramatic change in the political climate. The biggest single event from a tax standpoint was the California vote on Proposition 13. By a decisive margin, the people of that state approved a 57-percent cut in property taxes.

It quickly turned out that California voters were reflecting nationwide sentiment. In Massachusetts, Governor Michael S. Dukakis was defeated in the Democratic primaries by Edward J. King, a political unknown. King's victory was attributed to his support of the tax reduction. In New Jersey, Jeffrey Bell upset Clifford Case in the Republican senatorial primary. Bell said his success was due to all-out advocacy of tax cuts.

Meanwhile, new initiatives were being taken on the national tax front. The late Congressman William A. Steiger (R., Wisc.) said the capital shortage should be relieved by reducing the taxes of people who invested in business. The capital gains tax, which had been increased 49 percent in 1969, should be reduced to 25 percent. The aim was to encourage people to buy stock. Equity financing is a little used source of capital but one, Steiger said, that is vitally important to new, innovative companies.

The tax question moved into broad, fundamental territory that year with the introduction of the Kemp-Roth bill. Sponsored by Congressman Jack Kemp (R., N. Y.) and Senator William Roth (R., Del.), this called for a 33-percent cut in personal income taxes in three stages. It wasn't just business that was hurting, said Jack Kemp; the whole private sector was being repressed by excessive taxation. Decisive cuts would bring a surge of activity. People would work harder. Money would move from safe shelters to high-risk, high-return ventures. People are faced with "an unrealistically heavy burden of taxation," said Kemp. "This issue is whether the cut will restore incentive to the worker, saver, and investor in America."

The Steiger amendment was first regarded as a lonely, offbeat gesture, but it quickly became evident that Steiger was tapping a vast pool of popular support. By September, his ideas were being written into the tax bill.

Even more dramatic was the effect of the Kemp-Roth bill on the fortunes of Jack Kemp. Before he proposed a 33-percent tax cut, Kemp was a congressman from Buffalo, N. Y., whose main distinction was the fading memory of his days as a pro football quarterback. Overnight, the tax issue transferred him into a Republican hero and a possible presidential candidate.

THE BENEFICIARIES OF FREE ENTERPRISE

Until the 1978 tax uprising, the income equality movement could be presented as a response to the yearnings of the masses. Egalitarians could argue that vast numbers of people were being victimized by the unfairness of the system. But in 1978 it became clear that what the masses were yearning for was the right to keep more of their hard-earned bucks.

The tax rebellion was due largely to the movement of most people into the middle income bracket. "The overwhelming majority of Americans are—actually, prospectively, or retrospectively—middle-class," wrote Irving Kristol. He chastised those who saw the California vote as a "self-serving rebellion of the 'affluent' against government spending which favors the poor and unfortunate."[4]

In a sense, however, the vote was precisely that. Most people are more affluent than they used to be. Most people have been well served by the system of uneven rewards. This point is conceded by many who argue for greater redistribution. "A family with an income at the national average of about $14,000 today [1976] has a command over goods and services that would have put it well into the top 10 percent of the pyramid in 1948," wrote Arthur Okun.[5]

The income pyramid isn't a pyramid anymore—there is no broad base of low income earners. In 1975, as shown in Figure 1, more than 66 percent of all families had incomes over $10,000, and 44 percent had incomes over $15,000. What this means, among other things, is that most people are now the sponsors rather than the beneficiaries of government social spending. To put it another way, redistribution of income through jobs created by the free enterprise system is more beneficial to most people than government redistribution.

Those who complain about the static state of income shares

FIGURE 1-1. Distribution of Families by Income Levels (in 1975 dollars)

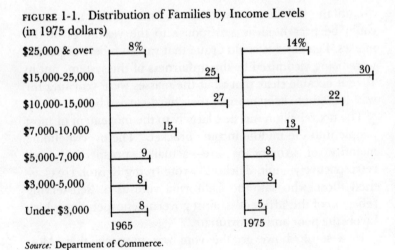

Source: Department of Commerce.

12

tend to neglect the dynamic change in the distribution of people by income levels. Writing in the *New York Times* (Feb. 19, 1978), Tom Wicker referred to the "oldest American myth—the golden dream of wealth for all of us." It is not a myth that the son of poor Jewish immigrants from Lithuania was head of DuPont in 1978. And it was not an isolated accident that Irving Shapiro rose to this eminence. People are constantly moving up in the United States—collectively and individually. The dividing point between the lowest fifth and the second lowest fifth on the income scale was four times higher in 1976 than in 1950. Inflation exaggerated the rise, but there was a real increase of nearly 170 percent.

In short, the unequal shares of a growing pie have elevated people's standard of living at all levels. It can be argued that those at the bottom have the greatest stake in preserving a system that has provided both growth and mobility. This point was at least partly recognized in 1978 by the National Association for the Advancement of Colored People (NAACP). In opposing no-growth energy policies, the NAACP noted that industrial expansion was one of the keys to providing opportunities for minorities.

The wisdom of this stand is brought out by examining recent industrial wage trends. Westinghouse Electric Corporation estimated these trends would provide a lifetime income of $6 million to the average employee who joined the company in 1978 and worked for forty years. Granted this projection implies a lot of inflation and a lot of job security, it also means the possibility of wealth for all can be more than myth. It is a certainty, if the free system is allowed to function. Repression of the system through high tax rates won't hurt those who already are wealthy, said David Rockefeller. The tax burden will be most painful for those who are striving to get ahead and move up.

THE PROBLEM OF POVERTY

All of which still leaves the problem of poverty. It doesn't seem right that some people are going without bare essentials while others are rolling in luxury. Shouldn't more be done for the poor? A great deal is already being done. Enough money is being spent to eliminate poverty. Because much of the transfer is in the form of benefits rather than cash, it is not counted in surveys of income. "If the food, housing and health benefits could be counted as good as cash, they would exceed the $12 billion counted as the poverty deficit," said Robert J. Lampman of the University of Wisconsin. He discusses how transfer payments change the actual incomes of those in the lowest bracket. "After we are done with all the taxing and transferring, both in money and in kind, the lowest fifth goes from something like 3 percent or so of prefisc income up to 10 percent or more of postfisc income."[6]

Others have come up with similar findings. Commenting on the amount of government social spending, Edgar K. Browning, professor of economics at the University of Virginia said, "It appears incredible that there was a single poor person left in the United States in 1973."[7] A 1977 study by the Congressional Budget Office confirmed that official figures understate income transfer and overstate the incidence of poverty. The study also came up with an estimate of $286 billion for social spending at all government levels in 1975.

THE COST OF ECONOMIC EQUALITY

Granted a lot is being done to alleviate poverty, is it not possible and desirable to do more? No, said Jack Kemp and others. In support of this contention, Kemp cited something called the Laffer Curve. Developed by Arthur B. Laffer, a

University of Southern California economist, the curve indicated taxation has reached the point of diminishing returns. Higher tax rates would kill the goose that lays the golden eggs; tax cuts would produce more tax dollars.

Even proponents of greater redistribution concede there would be some negative effects on efficiency and growth. Full equality would have too great an economic cost to be acceptable, said Arthur Okun, but he argued there is room for greater equality without a prohibitive loss of efficiency and growth. Jack Kemp and the Laffer Curve suggested otherwise. If the curve is valid, we have reached a point where redistributing a larger share of income is not only undesirable but impossible. The repressive effect of further taxation will reduce the dollars available to be redistributed.

Edgar Browning's studies indicated that the point of counterproductivity in greater redistribution had been reached. Further income transfer is not just a matter of soaking the rich, he said: there aren't enough rich people to do much good. Furthermore, "any major redistribution of income cannot avoid heavy taxation of families in the middle and upper-middle income range."

Recent history suggests this kind of taxation would depress the economy and reduce government tax revenues. The effect would be not a sharing of abundance, said Douglas Kenna, former president of the National Association of Manufacturers, but a "permanent rationing of scarcity."

There is ample evidence that most people prefer the present system of unequal rewards distributed in a free market. The lack of general discontent is illustrated by a Washington gag line: "Most people don't resent the two-martini lunch. They aspire to it." Given this widespread aspiration, it follows that economic equality can be achieved only by imposing the views of a minority against the will of the majority.

Of course, it doesn't necessarily follow that the majority is right. According to Professor Rawls, it is not enough for economic inequality to please and benefit most people. A system is unjust if benefits are achieved at the expense of abject poverty for even a few individuals.

Nevertheless, the principle of economic equality can be implemented only by minority control. This is dangerous business. The majority can be wrong, but it's unlikely it will go as far wrong as a minority. It's unlikely that a Hitler could be elected president of the United States; it's *not* unlikely, though, that a significant minority would vote for him.

Columbia University Professor Robert Nisbet says the push for equality is coming from a narrow minority consisting of "many intellectuals, leaders of special-interest groups, and a rising number of politicians and bureaucrats."[8] Nisbet feels this group has gone off the deep end. They have taken equality of opportunity to mean equality of result and condition, he charges.

This philosophy is unquestionably being applied on a number of fronts. A *Wall Street Journal* editorial (Sept. 28, 1978) noted that equality of condition is built into rules established by the Equal Employment Opportunity Commission and other government agencies. If a company's employment pattern does not conform to the prescribed pattern, the company is called on to show that its hiring practices have not placed undue stress on intelligence, personality, or common sense. The editorial went on to say that enforcers deny that application of EEO standards is an effective imposition of quotas, but "merely a method that will 'focus government enforcement on achieving tangible results.' "

THE COST OF GOVERNMENT INTERVENTION

Full economic equality cannot be achieved without government intervention. Operating in a free system, people will wind up in different positions on the economic scale. These differences can be prevented only by restricting freedom. "To check the growth of inequality, liberty must be sacrificed," wrote the Durants in *Lessons in History.*

Given a philosophy that everyone is to end up even, the most direct way of achieving this is for government to take over all income and divide it uniformly. Many believe the take-over process is advancing rapidly and that it does carry a threat to liberty. "What is to prevent a government already taking more than 40 percent of national income for one purpose or another from becoming a leviathan that ultimately devours all freedom?" asked G. Warren Nutter of the University of Virginia.[9]

The sacrifice of freedom would probably be in vain. It takes an optimistic view of human nature to believe government control of income would really produce equality—the prime beneficiaries would probably be the state bureaucrats.

But does it really follow that a government with economic control would elect to control all behavior? Could there not be a greater measure of equality without the repression of general liberty? Perhaps. But the tendency of government to regulate and dictate already has considerable impetus. The consumerists and the environmentalists are pressing for a greater government role in the decisions of individuals and companies. To a growing extent, income transfers are in the form of housing, medical care, and food stamps. These nonmoney benefits give to government the control not only of the amounts transferred but of the manner in which these sums will be spent.

All this is presented as protection and help for the defenseless masses. There is, no doubt, much sincere good will. However, there is also an implication that the average person is not wise enough to make his own decisions. There must be an elite group to govern behavior. Leaders of the black community are among those most resentful of the trend toward nonmoney transfers, which convey the message that poor people are not to be trusted with cash.

On the other side of the fence, egalitarians are saying, in effect, that the people of California, Massachusetts, and New Jersey are not to be trusted with votes, as such results as Proposition 13 show lack of wisdom. Robert Novak of American Enterprise Institute (AEI) said, according to the *Wall Street Journal* of September 8, 1978, that the appeal of Robert Kennedy for many liberals went beyond political issues. Images of Camelot entered in, he said. "It thus appears that many Democrats are secret royalists, touched by not a little loathing for the silent majority and by much noblesse oblige."

THE ROAD TO PROSPERITY

It is probably stretching things to say the tax debate of 1978 involved a choice between dictatorship or freedom. It is not far-fetched to say that 1978 left us still on the brink of a decisive commitment to socialism. The tax cuts of 1978 were somewhat greater than those proposed by the Carter administration. They fell far short of the 33-percent reduction called for by the Kemp-Roth bill. And with Social Security taxes going up in 1979, there was no net reduction for the average person.

This was unfortunate, because tax cuts are needed. One reason government is growing rapidly is that the private sector has not been growing rapidly. High unemployment has made it necessary to spend large sums for jobless pay and has created pressure for an expansion of public-service employment. Repeated recessions have provided ammunition for those who say the free process is not doing a good enough job of creating and distributing wealth.

All this is very sad, as we do know how to produce

prosperity today. It has been shown that the economy responds favorably to tax cuts. This is an exciting, momentous discovery, since one of the great failings of the free system has been its vulnerability to ups and downs. There need no longer be slumps and depressions and panics. In the 1978 tax debate, there was disagreement over the wisdom of producing prosperity. There was no disagreement over the fact that tax cuts would stimulate the economy.

As to why anyone would oppose such a desirable effect, the answer is, fear of inflation. Walter W. Heller, who was President Kennedy's economic adviser, and others warned that the Kemp-Roth bill would send prices zooming, that there would be too much demand for supply. Yet there is considerable evidence that modern inflation has little to do with demand: there was negligible inflation when demand was rising rapidly in the early sixties; there was a lot of inflation in the sluggish period from 1975 through 1978.

Prices have been going up in recent years because costs have been going up. A combination of lagging productivity and rapidly rising wages has pushed prices upward. It has been shown that pay rates are insensitive to demand; if anything, labor unions become more militant when things are bad. In terms of the effect on prices, it has also been shown that productivity reacts with reverse English to the law of supply and demand. The more demand is repressed, the less productive the system. Despite repeated demonstrations of these facts, government has stuck with the standard remedies for inflation. When prices are going up, demand is repressed by raising taxes or failing to cut taxes.

In this setting, there is a need to treat inflation as a cost phenomenon and to find new remedies. There is a need to create prosperity through broad tax relief. There is a need to recognize more clearly that prosperity is a good thing and recessions are bad things. If the private sector doesn't grow, the public sector will.

Chapter 2

THE CREATION OF WEALTH

"You can't distribute wealth you haven't created," said Fletcher Byrom, chairman of Koppers Company, Inc.

There is no way around this sequence of creation and distribution. It follows, then, that priority should go to the creative process; if distribution interferes with creation, distribution should be sacrificed. In the Soviet Union and other socialist countries, the adverse effects of reversing these priorities have been shown. Excessive emphasis on distribution has tended to retard the production of goods and services.

In heading down the same road of misplaced emphasis, the United States is moving away from the best system ever devised for creating wealth. The level of affluence in this country attests to the superiority of our system. The recent lag in productivity suggests we have gotten away from the ideal mix of creation and distribution.

The case against further redistribution of wealth rests very heavily on the assertion that the free market system of the United States has, indeed, done a superior job of creating abundance. To most people, including many who advocate further redistribution, this superiority is self-evident; however, the point is so important it should be documented.

There is ample statistical backing for the claim of superiority. It can also be shown there is a pattern of greater progress in free-market countries than in countries where there is a high degree of state control.

A CROSS-CULTURAL EXAMPLE

Before getting into numbers, it may be useful to offer a few firsthand observations and impressions. To me, at least, the best way to appreciate the performance of the United States system is to visit other countries.

A few years ago, I traveled to a place called Puerto Ordaz (Santo Tomè de Guayana) in Venezuela, an area located about 300 miles southeast of Caracas and the center of a big industrial expansion. To attract and house workers, the government had built high-rise apartments, many of them empty at the time of my visit; it had been impossible to collect the skills and hardware for finishing the interiors.

The gaps in the economy showed up again when a construction worker contacted me. He had been trying for a week to do something about a passport that had been lost or stolen. His attempts to call the U. S. embassy in Caracas had been unsuccessful. The phone system simply didn't work. (Officials of the construction company accepted the communications snarl philosophically. When there was an important business call to be made, they explained, a team was set up to take turns dialing.)

Back in Caracas a few days later, I was able to reach the U. S. embassy. The State Department said representatives would be visiting Puerto Ordaz in the next week and that if the construction worker could present his birth certificate, the passport matter would be straightened out. I then flew back to Pittsburgh and called the construction company, advising

21

them of the situation. They called the worker's family and got the birth certificate. A company official was flying to Venezuela the next day. He was able to get the birth certificate to Caracas in time for the embassy visit.

The point is, all problems of communications and movement disappeared when I was back in the United States. Two routine phone calls. Somebody jumped in the family car and delivered the certificate to downtown Pittsburgh. Someone else jumped in a jet, and a few hours later the birth certificate was in a South American outpost.

Venezuela is making a valiant, intelligent effort to turn oil riches into a lasting production base. But you don't realize until you're out of the United States the physical resources at your disposal here. It's not a question of money. No amount of money could buy good phone service in Venezuela.

In spite of the free market's record in producing abundance, most developing countries have gone to state-oriented systems with emphasis on avoiding profiteering and concentrations of wealth. This is a paradox, because it is these developing nations that should have the greatest concern for creating wealth. "In such countries," said Irving Kristol, "the alleviation of poverty is utterly dependent on economic growth. There is never enough money among the small number of wealthy citizens to make a significant dent in the poverty of the masses."[1]

In any country, you must have a lot of chickens before there is a chicken in every pot. Again, the great accomplishment of the American system is that it has produced large quantities of goods and services. The great failure of socialism has been its inability to create wealth.

"While governments are good at distributing abundance, they are not very effective at dealing with scarcity," said David Roderick, president of United States Steel Corp. While it isn't clear to me that governments are all that good at distributing wealth, they certainly have failed to create abundance.

Getting back to the passport example, instant communications were available in the United States because telephone and telegraph companies have nearly $150 billion worth of communications equipment. As measured by supplier sales, there was a $7 billion addition to the system in 1978.

The documents needed to replace the passport were quickly conveyed to downtown Pittsburgh because practically everyone in the United States has a car. There were 110 million autos registered in 1976. That came to roughly one car for every two persons. In the lowest income bracket— under $3000—more than 5 percent of the families owned two cars.[2] The passport material could be flown from Pittsburgh to Caracas on short notice because the United States has the world's leading aerospace industry. Over 20,000 civilian aircraft were built in 1978. These were worth $6.8 billion.

Air travel provides a number of interesting sidelights. When you leave this country, you board the plane through an enclosed ramp that extends out from the terminal building. When you arrive in Tokyo or Hamburg or Caracas, you debark out on the air field. Busses then take you to the terminal. This is not a big thing, but it makes you aware you have come from a more affluent country and are arriving in a less affluent one. Another point that registers is the presence of Boeing 707s, 727s and 747s. Over 5,400 civilian aircraft were exported in 1978.

POST-WORLD WAR II REBUILDING

Also of interest in Tokyo or Düsseldorf are the signs that say IBM, or EXXON, or FORD. These are reminders of the role played by U. S. dollars and U. S. enterprise in rebuilding the Free World after World War II. The extent of this effort sometimes is forgotten. From 1945 through 1954, the net foreign aid of the U. S. government was around $50 billion. Much more important was the transfer of physical wealth. The United States sent $232 billion worth of machines, materials, and other goods abroad in the early postwar years.

During the Vietnam period, there was much criticism of the government for maintaining a guns-and-butter policy. Largely overlooked was the minor impact on the United States civilian economy of massive drains during the Marshall Plan and the Korean War days.

During World War II, there was rationing and there were shortages, but no one went without butter or a reasonable substitute. The war demonstrated the enormous capacity of the American system to turn out goods and services.

OUR GROSS NATIONAL PRODUCT

Our system's capability has not been fully used in recent years. Perverse economic policies have prevented a great deal of progress. Nevertheless, the United States is still the richest country in the world. Figure 2–1 shows that in 1976 the U.S. Gross National Product (GNP) was over $1.7 trillion. That compared with $921 billion for the Soviet Union and $1.65 trillion for the entire communist bloc.

Throughout the world, the contrast between progress in the free countries and lagging growth in communist countries is striking. Eastern Europe had a GNP of $316 billion in 1976. Western Europe had an output of $1.4 trillion. China, with its great population, had a GNP of $324 billion. Tiny Japan exceeded this by 74 percent.

"Wherever countries of comparable resources have run the race together," said former Secretary of State Henry Kissinger, "—Austria and Czechoslovakia, West and East Germany, Greece and Bulgaria, South and North Korea—the economy with a significant private sector has clearly done more in fulfilling the aspirations of its people than its socialist counterpart."

Despite the fits and starts of recent years, the United States continues to grow. U.S. GNP passed the trillion-dollar mark in 1971. By 1978, the nation's output was over two trillion. Inflation is obviously exaggerating the growth rate, but in real terms, the U. S. economy doubled between 1960 and 1978.

FIGURE 2-1. Gross National Product—1976 (U.S. dollar values[1] in billions)

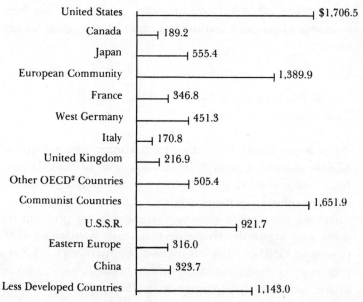

United States	$1,706.5
Canada	189.2
Japan	555.4
European Community	1,389.9
France	346.8
West Germany	451.3
Italy	170.8
United Kingdom	216.9
Other OECD[2] Countries	505.4
Communist Countries	1,651.9
U.S.S.R.	921.7
Eastern Europe	316.0
China	323.7
Less Developed Countries	1,143.0

[1]Based on 1976 average rates of exchange; Communist countries are converted to U.S. purchasing power equivalents.

[2]Organization for Economic Cooperation and Development.

Source: Department of Commerce; Organization for Economic Cooperation and Development.

On the other hand, the Soviet Union seems to be finding it increasingly difficult to get things on the right track. Writing in the Wall Street Journal (Oct. 5, 1978), Kenneth L. Adelman, formerly an assistant to the Secretary of Defense, said, "In economics, the U.S.S.R. has a slower growth rate than at any time since World War II. Its current Five Year Plan, which set embarrassingly unambitious goals, is nonetheless hopelessly behind schedule."

Time Magazine gave a similar report on the Russians (March 1, 1976). "Roughly 30 percent of the Soviet population is engaged in farming, compared to 5 percent in the U. S. No less than 31 percent of all investment under the new Five Year Plan has been allocated to agriculture. Yet, by the standards of other industrial nations, the U.S.S.R. has been incapable of properly feeding its people, even in good harvest times."

THE "PROBLEM" OF SWEDEN, THE EXAMPLE OF BRITAIN

On a per-capita basis, the 1976 United States GNP of $7,910 compared with $3,610 for Great Britain. Despite recent gains abroad, the U.S. had a higher per-capita output than any other large nation (figure 2–2).

Among the smaller nations, there is one big problem for those who argue the free enterprise case. Sweden's $9,000 per-capita GNP in 1976 was highest of any country. This is a problem to proponents of capitalism, because Sweden is one of the most socialistic countries in the Free World. If it is possible to generalize from the Swedish experience, then there is reason to take another look at socialism. A system which protects people from the jostling of the free market certainly has much to be said for it.

The Swedish experience cannot be dismissed, but it represents an awfully small sample. Sweden's total GNP was $74 billion in 1976, compared with $1.7 trillion for the United States. In view of the prevailing pattern in favor of private enterprise, it is not unreasonable to assume Sweden's success does not reflect the normal results of socialism. Finally,

FIGURE 2-2.   Per-Capita Gross National Product—1976 (U.S. dollar values[1] in billions)

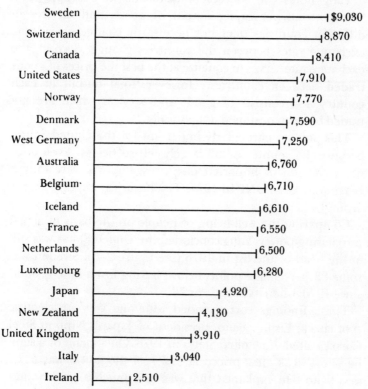

Sweden	$9,030
Switzerland	8,870
Canada	8,410
United States	7,910
Norway	7,770
Denmark	7,590
West Germany	7,250
Australia	6,760
Belgium	6,710
Iceland	6,610
France	6,550
Netherlands	6,500
Luxembourg	6,280
Japan	4,920
New Zealand	4,130
United Kingdom	3,910
Italy	3,040
Ireland	2,510

[1]Based on 1976 price and exchange rates.
Source: Organization for Economic Cooperation and Development.

Sweden's economy has looked less rosy in recent years. There are those who feel the adverse effects of socialism are starting to show up in the country.

All these arguments or excuses are really unnecessary, according to a study by Jai-Hoon Yang in the May, 1978, bulletin of the Federal Reserve Bank of St. Louis. Yang explains that the standard way of comparing nations is to convert the different outputs into dollars. This means relative positions are affected by exchange rates.

Yang notes two sources of distortion in this approach: "First, actual per capita output of goods and services in different countries does not necessarily change every time exchange rates between the countries change. Second, the exchange rate serves to equalize at the best the prices of goods traded between countries. However, total output in each country also consists of goods and services which are not traded but are consumed domestically."

This point is particularly important for the United States, because the country is still largely self-sufficient. Even after the escalation of imported oil prices, imports were only 8 percent of U. S. GNP in 1977. The historical import share is around 4 percent.

Comparing the well-being of people on the basis of actual purchasing power, Yang concluded the United States was still at the head of the list in 1976 (see figure 2–3). Sweden was some 23 percentage points below, having lost a little ground since 1970, when its parity was 78.

These findings corresponded with one very unscientific spot check. Eishiro Saito, president of Japan's Nippon Steel Corp., visited the United States in 1978. On a menu or a sign, he saw a steak meal priced at $2.70. "I thought it was $27," said Saito. He explained that was how much a steak would cost in Tokyo. His point was the same as Yang's: changes in currency rates don't really reflect what is happening inside countries.

Figures put out by the Organization for Economic Cooperation and Development (OECD) seem to support the view that the United States is still the most affluent nation. Figure 2–4 shows that this country has more telephones and television sets per person than any other. Our per-capita energy consumption is higher than any other country's except Luxembourg. We trail only New Zealand and Australia in per-capita protein input. Only Japan has a higher percentage of children from 15 to 19 going to school full time.

On this last point, it's interesting that the 72 percent U.S. educational enrollment compared with 57.1 percent in Sweden and under 44 percent for Great Britain. One of the raps against socialism in Britain is that the rapid diversion of people and money into public service has not improved the service. "There is no reason in terms of population structure why resources should have been moved from industry into education and the various welfare services so extraordinarily quickly in Britain," wrote Bacon and Eltis. "The availability of hospital beds per head of the population actually fell 11 percent in Britain from 1961 to 1971, and it increased 10

FIGURE 2-3. International Comparisons of Per-Capita Output via Purchasing Power Parties—1976 (U.S.=100)

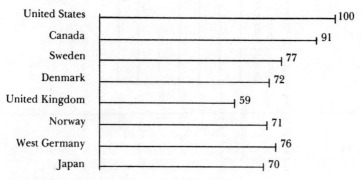

Source: Jai-Hoon Yang, *Federal Reserve Review,* May 1978.

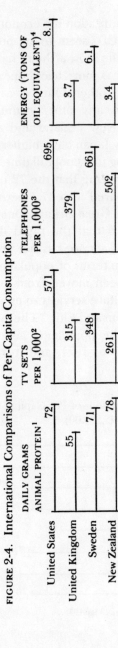

FIGURE 2-4. International Comparisons of Per-Capita Consumption

	DAILY GRAMS ANIMAL PROTEIN[1]	TV SETS PER 1,000[2]	TELEPHONES PER 1,000[3]	ENERGY (TONS OF OIL EQUIVALENT)[4]
United States	72	571	695	8.1
United Kingdom	55	315	379	3.7
Sweden	71	348	661	6.1
New Zealand	78	261	502	3.4
Japan	33	233	405	3.1
West Germany	56	305	317	4.2
Canada	65	366	572	8.5

[1]1975. [2]1974. [3]1975. [4]1975.

Source: Organization for Economic Cooperation and Development.

percent in West Germany and 15 percent in Italy, falling slightly in France."[3]

This example suggests the efficiency of socialism in distributing wealth is open to question. With regard to creating wealth, there is no contest. "In comparison with any other production system in man's history or any blueprint currently on the drawing board, the American economy must get a high performance rating," wrote Arthur Okun. "Judging it as a system of production, I see no case for trading it in for a new model."

OUR RECENT RECORD OF GROWTH

Judging the system on the basis of how things used to be, there are also grounds for rejoicing. As figure 2–5 shows,

FIGURE 2-5. Median Income (in 1976 dollars)

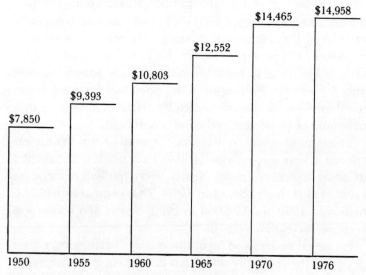

Source: Department of Commerce, Bureau of the Census.

median family income in 1976 was $14,958. Adjusting for inflation, that was up 38 percent from 1960 and 90 percent from 1950.

Our rate of progress has slowed in recent years, but there has still been an enormous amount. In 1976, the average person was nearly twice as well off as he was in 1950.

These broad numbers translate into an improvement in almost every aspect of living. From 1960 to 1976, for example, according to the Conference Board's *A Guide to Consumer Markets*, per-capita food consumption rose 10.9 percent. We complain about rising food prices, but we can't conceive of a situation in which it is physically impossible to get all the food we want. Yet, there are still famines in the world. The problem in the United States is usually one of surplus food production.

Twenty-one million housing units were built in the United States from 1960 to 1976. That was almost a third of the total occupied at the end of the period. Measured in constant dollars, as seen in figure 2–6, U. S. spending rose from 1960 to 1976 by these amounts: housing, 100 percent; household appliance, 112 percent; radio and TV, 452 percent; medical care, 203 percent. In the same span, the U. S. population rose only 20 percent. Netting out the population increase, living standards—at least, as measured by dollars spent—rose by a minimum of 80 percent in the four areas cited.

These numbers mean that a vast amount of real wealth was created. There was enough left over after needs were satisfied to provide luxury items. Nearly seven million Americans could afford to go abroad in 1976. That compared with 1.6 million in 1960 and 676,000 in 1950. Nearly $66 billion was spent on recreation in 1976.

For a real understanding of this country's affluence, go out to one of the shopping malls that have sprung up overnight across the country. (There were 1.9 million retail establishments in 1972—up 9.7 percent from 1967.) At these malls, every conceivable product is available in abundance. Food, clothes, shoes, calculators, TV sets are yours just for the exchange of a few paper bills.

After your visit, read some of the horror stories about shopping in the U.S.S.R. "The shortages are so commonplace that people will join any queue they see and then ask what it is for," reported *Time* (March 1, 1976). "Soap, toothpaste, perfumes, detergents, toilet paper, hairpins, and matches were of inferior quality or not available at all."

THE QUALITY OF LIFE

There is, of course, criticism of the American system precisely because it is so effective in creating wealth. We are told production should be slowed in the interest of enhancing the quality of life.

FIGURE 2-6. Real Growth in Consumption Expenditures—1960-1975 (based on 1975 dollars; 1960=100)

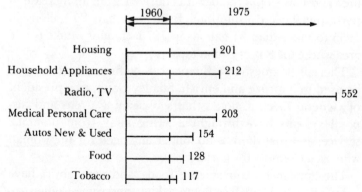

Source: Department of Commerce.

Variations of this idea have been advanced over the years. Thirty or forty years ago, there would be occasional comments from Europe to the effect that Americans were cluttering up their lives with material things that didn't bring happiness. When the Europeans succeeded in accumulating a little clutter of their own, there was less of this talk.

In the days when there were holy men, people were advised that true contentment came from mortifying the flesh and liberating the spirit. This is a legitimate point of view, but not one that is embraced by many of us. The ascetic life is particularly unpopular when it is forced on people.

The modern version of spiritualism calls for us to get back to tilling the soil and pumping water and walking in the woods. These are appealing notions. They aren't practical—and when you get down to specifics, they aren't what people want. "Some housewife with two children—all she needs is one day without her automatic washer and she's in trouble," said one General Electric executive. It might be added that over half the U. S. families with income under $5,000 had automatic washers in 1974. Over 92 percent of these families had TV sets.

You may doubt that television has added to the quality of life. You may doubt the benefits derived from an increase in per-capita beer consumption from less than 25 gallons in 1955 to more than 31 gallons in 1976. (Liquor intake is one area where the Soviet Union tops us.)

There is no question affluence can be misused. It can also be used to improve and enrich. Stanley Gault, vice president of General Electric, noted that self-cleaning ovens and disposal systems have brought a swing away from domestic service, and that there is no longer any need for the woman who used to empty the garbage.

The appliances, convenience foods, and new fabrics have led to virtually labor-free homemaking, and some women are doubtless using their spare time to eat chocolates and read movie magazines. But many are not. The extraordinary popularity of home sewing, for instance, has far more to do with creative use of leisure time than with cost-saving.

At the height of the student protests in the late 1960s, the graduating class at Penn State was addressed by Eric A. Walker, retired president of that university. Walker challenged the student notion that the past generation has been hung up on the shoddier forms of materialism. "These—your parents and grandparents—are the people who within just five decades—1919–1969—have by their work increased your life expectancy by approximately 50 percent—who, while cutting the work day by a third, have more than doubled per capita output. These are the people who gave you a healthier world than they found. Because they gave you the best, you are the tallest, healthiest, brightest, and probably the best-looking generation to inhabit the land. And because they were materialistic, you will work fewer hours, learn more, have more leisure time, travel to more places, and have more of a chance to follow your heart's desire."

THE NEED FOR MORE GROWTH

There has been great progress, but there is an urgent need for further improvement. In 1976 there were nearly 25 million Americans in the poverty bracket. Other nations may be worse off, but the United States is still far from perfection. In this setting, a reversal of growth would not lead to rustic tranquility. In a nation of over 200 million, it would lead to more slums. And city slums are not calculated to bring out the best in people. A government panel concluded that the urban poor are "burdened with an enormous set of circumstances that pull many toward crime."

Elimination of these circumstances calls for the creation of more real wealth. We can juggle income shares all we like, but unless there is a bigger pie, there will be no upward movement. Unless there are more nice homes, the percentage of the population living in slums won't change. In a static economy, the slum dwellers will very likely be the same individuals now living in poverty.

Among those acutely aware of this probability are officials of the National Advancement for the Advancement of Colored People (NAACP). The organization reacted strongly when the Carter administration put out an energy program with emphasis on repressing demand rather than on expanding supply.

"If there is no adequate supply of energy available," said the NAACP executive director, "then industry will not expand, new jobs will not be created, and we'll end up with joblessness of epidemic proportions in the black community. . . . We are saying to the President . . . that there must be a greater effort put on expanding sources for energy. We cannot live in a no-growth economy; we cannot live in a situation where . . . jobs are not being created."

The NAACP later said its position had been distorted. However, it should not be surpirising that the black community sees little future for itself in a no-growth economy. The lack of progress for blacks after the Civil War was partly due to the static southern rural economy. "For the southern rural black, the advent of industrial society meant a measure of economic emancipation," wrote Bayard Rustin, president of the A. Philip Randolph Institute.[4]

Rustin noted that the no-growth advocates were frequently the same people who called for a more equitable social order. "There is a glaring contradiction between their opposition to growth on the one hand and their avowed support for a more equal social order on the other. . . . The most essential social changes that are necessary to bring about more social equity and racial advancement are not in the direction of a pastoral or communal fantasy world. We are going to need jobs and not merely jobs in low-paying, labor intensive fields. It is going to take economic growth and lots of it if we are to realize the ideals of equality, cooperation, and economic justice."

Rustin rejected the argument that progress in the United States was depriving less developed countries of their share of the world's wealth. "In fact, economic development of the Third World is inextricably tied to continuous high rates of growth by the Western Nations, the United States most particularly. The new nations," said Rustin, "subscribe to John Kennedy's statement that 'a rising tide lifts all boats.' "[5]

It is not a new thing for oppressed people to see their salvation in the industrial tide. The industrial revolution of the nineteenth century did not enslave men; it liberated them, says Paul Johnson, former editor of the *New Statesman*.

Writing in the Wall Street Journal (Sept. 29, 1976), Johnson noted, "The factory system, however harsh it may have been, was the road to freedom for millions of agricultural workers," said Johnson. "Not only did it offer them escape from rural poverty, which was deeper and more degrading than anything experienced in the city, but it allowed them to move from status to contract, from a stationary place in a static society . . . to a mobile place in a dynamic one."

I don't think it is necessary to prove that growth and progress are good things. This book assumes they are and is concerned primarily with ways of promoting the material well-being of the nation and of individuals at all levels.

THE NO-GROWTH MOVEMENT

It is necessary to digress, however, because growth is being blocked. This is not because of popular oppostion. What makes the no-growth movement formidable is the ready means available to anyone who doesn't like power plants, or steel mills, or refineries. The regulations on health, safety, and pollution provide all kinds of opportunities to erect roadblocks.

Because of the long clearance procedure, it now takes twelve years to bring a nuclear power plant on stream. The diffculties of the procedure have helped to choke off new construction. In fact, the nuclear industry has experienced a virtual moratorium on new orders since mid-1974. This helps explain why the National Electric Reliability Council predicts general power shortages by the mid-1980s.

The country is already in a deficit position on steel, and no relief is in sight. United States Steel Corporation began in early 1977 to seek environmental approval for a new mill on Lake Erie. By early 1979, the clearance process was still in an early stage and the outcome very doubtful. Nonapproval of the plant, said former U. S. Steel Chairman E. B. Speer, will mean it's impossible to build a new steel plant anywhere in the United States as no location is more favorable from an environmental standpoint than the Lake Erie site.

This situation figures to get worse. Environmentalists are aggressively pursuing their aims. In one 1978 suit, the Environmental Defense Fund was asking the courts to void all construction permits issued since August of 1977. "They've been suing us every week," muttered an official of the Environmental Protection Agency (EPA). The legal pressure is making EPA super cautious and slow.

Under the Clean Air amendments of 1977, the states were given until the middle of 1979 to have new implementation programs in place. In the absence of such plans, no new construction permits may be issued.

In terms of environmental quality, the no-growth people are really cutting their own throats. We aren't going back to a pastoral Utopia. There are going to be plants and cities in the year 2000. Unless there is balanced growth, however, there are going to be shortages in vital areas.

What this will mean is shown by looking at just one cleanup program. Republic Steel Corp. has spent $19 million on a water treatment plant at Canton, Ohio. For the foundation, two-and-a-half miles of steel piling were sunk. Three miles of underground piping will carry 10,000 gallons a minute. The water plant will use enough power to heat and light 1,100 homes. It will cost $3 million a year to operate.

If the no-growth people have their way, there simply won't be the power and materials to put into this kind of cleanup program. The choice will be between providing the necessities of life or providing pollution abatement. This choice isn't fantasy—it's already been forced in some cases. The decision at that point will be the same as the decision made in 1978 when the coal strike created a power shortage. Plants in the affected areas were told to forget about running their cleanup systems. The power was needed to keep homes heated and lighted.

MORE GROWTH, LESS POLLUTION

In short, the ultimate effect on no-growth policies will be to increase pollution. On the other hand, the effect of vigorous growth would probably be to reduce pollution. In terms of economics and technology, it is much easier to smog-proof a new plant than an old one.

Retarded growth is one of the reasons the steel industry has had such difficult pollution problems. Shipments in 1977 were less than shipments in 1965. Steelmaking capacity in 1974 was about the same as capacity in 1960. In the absence of growth and expansion, steel companies have been in the position of having to clean up existing facilities and plants. It

39

is almost impossible to prevent emissions from an old coke oven. And at a recent check, 45 percent of the nation's coke was coming from ovens that had been around twenty years or more.

From a financial standpoint, environmental spending on an existing facility is a straight loss. The loss is particularly painful when the facility is near the end of its useful life.

Much more feasible and attractive are projects involving brand-new plants. Here, the cost of abatement can be offset by added volume and increased efficiency. Equipment can be designed from the outset with space for control devices. The word "attractive" is appropriate, because modern plants are being built not simply to control emissions but to provide positive beautification. One example is the mill built by the Steel Company of Canada, Ltd., on Lake Erie near Nanticoke, Ontario. In addition to the latest pollution controls and a dock that permits the normal flow of shellfish, the new mill has been landscaped like a park. There are lawns and lakes around the work areas. A green belt circles the rim. Rolling hills have been shaped to shield the countryside from industrial sights and sounds.

Starting from scratch with a new facility, a company can employ technology that is impractical for older operations. A process called dry quenching has been developed for coke batteries. Instead of cooling coke by dousing it with water, this method transfers heat from dry coke in an enclosed chamber. The captured heat is used to make steam. Apart from eliminating quenching emissions, the dry practice gives significant energy savings.

In a new plant, related facilities can be designed to make use of the waste heat. The quenching station can be built from the outset with the dry method in mind. Under these conditions, dry quenching comes close to economic feasibility. It does not make economic sense when it is necessary to go in and tear down a lot of existing equipment or when the battery is too old to comply with emission standards anyway.

Because of existing regulations, any new industrial facility will be equipped with devices that catch practically all emissions. At Houston, Texas, Armco Steel Corporation first equipped its electrical furnaces with a system that caught about ninety percent of the emissions. Armco later installed hoods over the furnaces and an additional filtering system. That increased control efficiency to something like 99 percent. This degree of cleanliness is now standard and uncontested.

The point is that the area of dispute on pollution control is now very narrow. Company people may gripe and groan, but it is required that any basic process will have all kinds of canopies, scrubbers, precipitators, and filters.

Armco and others balked, however, when they were told they had to do something about the fugitive wisps that escaped the two control systems. "That incremental amount will cost about $30 per pound of dust recovered," said John Barker, director of environemntal engineering for Armco. Company people argue that the enormous cost is not commensurate with the small benefits, and that the money is being taken away from more useful and important functions.

To fight poverty and pollution means we must create more wealth. We must grow. Nevertheless, we have set up a regulatory process that allows growth to be strangled and the no-growth people to run wild.

Much of this activity will force more decisions like the one made during the 1978 coal strike. Unfortunately, it takes something like a power shortage to show the difference between niceties and necessities, and until a crisis occurs, the decision is being made in favor of niceties—housing projects blocked so as not to interfere with the breeding cycles of alligators and whooping cranes, for example.

Bayard Rustin is one who has difficulty reconciling the lofty pretensions of the no-growth people with their blindness or indifference to human consequences. Rustin speaks of a "scarcely camouflaged elitism." Similar comments come from L. T. Papay, director of research and development for Southern California Edison. After spending ten years and $20 million, Southern California and other utilities gave up on the coal-fired Kaparowits project in Utah. There was never a popular drive against the power plant, said Papay. The plant was held up "by the actions of a select, elite group, who, for a simple filing fee, can bring a multi-million project to its knees."

THE RESOURCES FOR GROWTH

When considering the question of land preservation, it's worth remembering that in many ways nature is tough and adaptable. Nature is a formidable adversary, and man is not always victor in his struggle against it. In our own country, human beings really aren't crowding out other forms of animal and vegetable life. The problem is just the opposite: most of the people are huddled together on 3 percent of the national acreage, and nearly half the land is wilderness, swamp, and desert. During the Sixties, five million acres were added to the national system of parks and wilderness.

The land pattern is apparent when you travel by air on a clear day. Even such populous states as Pennsylvania and New Jersey have an amazing amount of unoccupied wilderness. If recent population trends are any indication, this land will remain unoccupied. The population of the United States increased by twenty million from 1960 to 1968. In the next eight years, the increase was only fifteen million. The population is now growing less than one percent a year. The rate of increase in 1976 was less than half the peaks of the Fifties and the Sixties.

The problem of government regulation will be treated in more detail in Chapter 6. Suffice it to say here that the limits on growth are philosophical and administrative and not, as some people contend, physical or technical. It is true that there are limits to the world's supply of fossil fuel. It is also true the sperm whale was once the prime source of lighting oil. Had there been no technological change, the nation would have blacked out.

If today's fuel requirements seem formidable, consider how an accurate forecast of U.S. food requirements would have looked in 1800. At that time, the society had to be largely agrarian to raise food for a population of five million. There would have been despair if people had known the nation would have to feed 211 million by 1974. There would have been disbelief if someone had said all the food would come from a farm group made up of only 4.4 percent of the population.

Sooner or later, indeed, the world is going to run out of oil. But there should be enough coal to keep us going until completely new energy sources are developed. "World resources of coal total over eight trillion tons," said Dell H. Adams, vice president of exploration for Consolidation Coal Company. "This is equivalent to 33 trillion barrels of oil, or ten or twenty times the estimate of ultimately recoverable oil resources in the world. In the United States, we have recoverable coal resources of about 1.5 trillion tons—sufficient to meet our domestic needs for thousands of years." (The U. S. Geological Survey assumes another trillion and a half tons have yet to be discovered.)

The United States has a 100-billion-ton iron ore resource and a proven reserve of seventeen billion tons. Domestic iron ore consumption is running around 130 million tons a year.

This country imports 90 percent of its bauxite, but there are vast deposits of lower-grade aluminum-bearing clays within the United States. "The United States has unlimited domestic aluminiferrous resources," said Carl H. Cotterill, assistant director of the U. S. Bureau of Mines. "The United States has been generously endowed with minerals and with proper attention to the various factors . . . there is no cause for alarm at the danger of running out of minerals. As a matter of fact, despite the greatly increased rate of mineral useage in recent decades, most world mineral reserves in terms of years supply are at their highest levels."

The same paper noted that the U. S. share of world consumption and production has been shrinking. In 1960, the United States produced 50 percent of all plastics. By 1977, the U. S. share was down to 29 percent. Our shares of aluminum and steel production have likewise become smaller slices of the totals.

With regard to material supplies, nothing is actually consumed. The various elements are simply converted into other forms. In coming years, recycling will account for a growing portion of our material needs. We will be recovering not only the waste materials generated each year but past accumulations.

According to a study by Robert B. Nathan Associates, Inc., the United States has piled up 270 million tons of unused steel scrap in the past twenty years. Adding the carry-over from earlier periods, the Nathan study placed the total scrap inventory at 636 million tons in 1975. That equaled about six years' steel consumption in the United States.

These figures are disputed, but there is unquestionably a large supply of waste material waiting to be tapped. Because of recycling, the Aluminum Company of America (Alcoa) recently revised its estimate of future supply. "A year and a half ago, we were projecting a shortfall in the 1978 to 1980 time frame," said Harry M. Georn, Alcoa's general manager of corporate planning. "Today, we are looking at a balanced supply picture through 1980 with a slight shortfall in 1981." He explained that recycling had changed the outlook. "We have seen a recent and large percentage increase in old scrap recovery."

Alcoa's can recovery program netted the company 94 million pounds in 1977. From all sources, the company took in 329 million pounds of old aluminum. Apart from conserving minerals, the use of scrap reduces aluminum's power consumption 95 percent. There is a similar saving in steel when iron ore is replaced with scrap.

All these things are piddling compared to developments being discussed in matter-of-fact tones by scientists. "In the remainder of this century," said Klaus P. Heiss, president of ECON, Inc., "and certainly in the years of the twenty-first century, the viability of space as an efficient, clean, and close to inexhaustible energy source for all mankind will have been established."

Heiss said the world's total fuel supply, built up by the sun's action over millions of years, has an energy content only ten times greater than the earth's intake of solar energy in a single day. The technical and economic feasibility of space stations to collect energy is a certainty today, he said. No big breakthroughs are required.

But there are breakthroughs. In October of 1978, Westinghouse Electric Corporation announced "the achievement of high efficiencies in the conversion of solar energy to electricity in solar photovoltaic cells made of silicon." A month or so earlier, Westinghouse came out with an improved superconductive magnet. This was a step toward solving the containment problems of fusion power generation—and fusion is another potential source of limitless energy.

These are just the things we know will be coming. If history is any guide, much of our progress will come from things that are not even being dreamed about today. Go back fifty years and think how a description of the future would have sounded: the atom bomb, the landing on the moon with hundreds of millions watching on home TV sets, pocket-sized calculators, computers, micro-circuitry—these things would not have been accepted even as plausible science fiction.

The recurring problem in the United States has been an inability to use the potentials available from new technology. Yet, somehow there is always an underlying fear that we are asking too much of the system. This fear has resulted in economic mismanagement. The problem is being compounded today by the notion that progress necessitates damage to the environment and humans, and hence that progress itself is immoral.

This notion can't be dismissed, because it is having such impact. But if the issue is stated in clear terms, we don't believe many people favor going without automobiles, refrigerators, and electric lighting. We think most people want progress. The American system is the most progressive on earth.

Chapter 3

THE FREE MARKET DISTRIBUTION OF WEALTH

Income in the United States is distributed mostly by the workings of the free market. In recent years, this initial distribution has been modified by government redistribution. There is pressure today for much greater redistribution of income because, it's argued, the unregulated process gives results that are unfair and arbitrary.

The danger in further redistribution of income through government is that it will weaken the private system to a critical extent. Before traveling further down the road of income redistribution, therefore, it seems a good idea to look at how well or how poorly the free market has performed.

The fact is, the system of uneven rewards has produced a massive elevation of people's standard of living. The extent of the uplift will be shown by statistics, but the best proof comes from personal observation. Looking back, the average person can see ancestors who lived in poverty. Most of us don't have to look very far back. Today, most of us find ourselves in the middle-income bracket. We enjoy better living standards than did our parents or grandparents. Looking around, the average person can see friends and associates who fit the same pattern.

Some of the affluence we observe represents achievement and success. The United States of America is still the land of opportunity. Progress is distributed by giving people a chance to realize their potential. The continued upward infusion of talent is one of the secrets of U. S. success. However, much of today's affuence comes from changes in income distribution. A profound change has been the transformation of the plant worker into a middle-income person. A man can now work with his hands in the United States and earn $20,000 or $30,000 a year.

This point was brought home to me on a flight to Florida. We normally travel tourist, but since the tourist section was full, we were traveling in the first-class section. Among those adding to the crowded condition of the plane was the gardener from our development. We live in a garden apartment cooperative which has a crew to mow lawns and keep things tidy. Our gardener was going to Florida for two weeks, and he didn't look out of place: about half the male passengers had weathered skin and the muscular look of men who work with their hands.

I wasn't surprised at this. My own lifetime income is only a few notches above that of a steelworker with a reasonable amount of skill. That isn't a bad economic ball park. In 1977, the average earnings of steelworkers were over $9 an hour. If a man worked full time, that came to over $18,000 a year.

With medical insurance and other benefits thrown in, the steelworker package had a cost of $14.11 an hour in April of 1978. On a yearly basis, that was over $28,000. The union estimates the contract signed in 1977 will raise annual pay in the lowest job class by $4,000 over three years. The steelworkers have done quite well, but to some extent their gains simply reflect the general trend. Median family income in 1976 was just under $15,000, up 90 percent from 1950.

EMPLOYEES' GAINS

Comparing the progress of company owners to company employees, the employees have been the winners. In 1977, as figure 3–1 shows, the amount of national income to be distributed was over $1.5 trillion. Of this, 76 percent went to the compensation of employees. That compared with 71 percent in 1960 and 65 percent in 1950. After-tax corporate profits in 1977 were 6.5 percent of national income. That was down from 8.9 percent in 1960 and 10.5 percent in 1950. The trend has clearly been toward a larger share of the total for compensation and a smaller share for profit. This split is important because compensation accounts for the biggest slice of personal income. In 1976, this slice was 75 percent of personal income.

By way of contrast, government transfer payments accounted for only 13 percent of total personal income in 1977. In other words, distribution of income is still determined primarily by how much people are paid for working. This is hardly surprising, since over 90 percent of the work force is employed, even during recessions.

The broad figures on compensation don't tell anything except that owners, who tend to be wealthy people, are not grabbing an inordinate share of the pie. It could be that the enlarged portion going to compensation is largely a reflection of salaries for people like the Rockefeller brothers.

Oddly enough, the Labor Department began keeping regular tabs on income by job levels only a few years ago.

Providing some historical data, a 1977 study showed that the salaries of managers and administrators rose at an annual rate of 6.5 percent from 1967 to 1976 (figure 3–2). In the same span, the wages of blue-collar operators rose 8 percent, craft workers moved up 6.9 percent a year, and farm workers

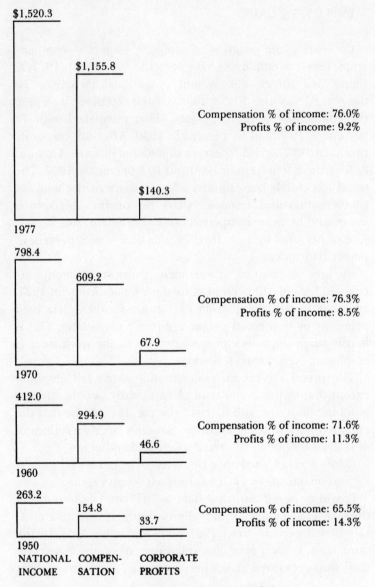

FIGURE 3-1. Compensation and Profit Shares of National Income (in billions of dollars)

$1,520.3

$1,155.8

$140.3

Compensation % of income: 76.0%
Profits % of income: 9.2%

1977

798.4

609.2

67.9

Compensation % of income: 76.3%
Profits % of income: 8.5%

1970

412.0

294.9

46.6

Compensation % of income: 71.6%
Profits % of income: 11.3%

1960

263.2

154.8

33.7

Compensation % of income: 65.5%
Profits % of income: 14.3%

1950
NATIONAL   COMPEN-   CORPORATE
INCOME   SATION   PROFITS

Source: Department of Commerce, Bureau of Economic Analysis.

gained at an annual rate of 8.4 percent. The pattern for the last few years is similar. In the year ending March, 1978, blue-collar wages went up 7.8 percent. Salaried employees got a 6.3-percent boost.

These numbers understate the gains for both wage and salaried people. The Conference Board, which gathers business information, reported in 1976 that top executives received bonuses in 78 percent of the manufacuring companies surveyed. The median bonus was 42 percent of salary for the three most highly paid executives in each type of business.

In the blue-collar ranks, fringe benefits are a large and

FIGURE 3-2. Annual Average Change of Median Weekly Earnings—1967-1976

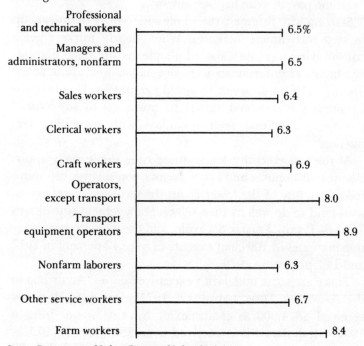

Professional and technical workers	6.5%
Managers and administrators, nonfarm	6.5
Sales workers	6.4
Clerical workers	6.3
Craft workers	6.9
Operators, except transport	8.0
Transport equipment operators	8.9
Nonfarm laborers	6.3
Other service workers	6.7
Farm workers	8.4

Source: Department of Labor, Bureau of Labor Statistics.

growing portion of total compensation. Of the $13 hourly employment cost in steel in 1977, fringes accounted for $4.36, or 34 percent. According to the Bureau of Labor Statistics (BLS), hourly earnings rose 8.7 percent in the year ending August, 1978, whereas hourly compensation rose 9.2 percent.

There is one fairly obvious reason to expect compensation to increase at the same rate for blue-collar and management people. The increases negotiated by unions are always considered excessive by companies. It would not be expected that top executives would give salaried employees larger hikes. On the other hand, companies can't give salaried people smaller increases than hourly workers. If they did, foremen would soon be making less than the crews under them. (With overtime pay, this can happen anyway.)

Starting with foremen, the whole supervisory chain goes up in step with union increases. When hourly workers get a cost-of-living increase, salaried people get the same percentage boost. If differentials were not maintained, those at the lower end of the salary scale would join unions. People in the bargaining unit would refuse to move up to supervisory positions—a refusal seen nowadays with increasing frequency.

At the top executive levels, these rules don't really apply. Because of bonuses and other factors, top salaries can move independently of the lower chain. In recovery years, executives tend to do well by themselves. Management consultants Towers, Perrin, Forster & Crosby said the median compensation increases of 100 chief executives were 12 percent in 1977 and 14.5 percent in 1976.

There are some outlandish executive salaries. According to the *New York Times* (April 17, 1977), David J. Mahoney received $814,000 as chairman of Norton Simon, Inc., in 1977; Meshulam Riklis received over $900,000 in 1975 as chairman of Rapid American Corporation, which lost $9 million that year; Harold S. Geneen of ITT pulled down a cool $846,000 in 1976. Stockholders are starting to complain about excessive compensation for executives. One lawsuit imposed limits on the take-home pay of David Mahoney. Another brought a small reduction in the 1975 compensation of Meshulam Riklis.

But for most employees, wage and salary movements are linked. Fewer than 30 percent of all workers are unionized, but, as has been noted, there is a direct carry-over to the nonunion portions of organized companies. If a company is not organized or has an independent union, it will make sure it matches the industry pattern.

Even those completely outside the sphere of unions are affected by area and industry patterns. Electrical manufacturers try to avoid building a plant near a steel mill; they don't want to compete for workers against the very high steel wages.

CONSTANT INCOME SHARES

The impetus for pay hikes for many people comes from the unionized industrial workers. This tends to assure at least a constant share for those in the lower echelons. The raw figures on income distribution suggest shares have been fairly constant. In 1950 the lowest fifth of all families earned 4.5 percent of U. S. aggregate income. The share of the same fifth went up to 5.4 percent in 1970 and 1976. The income share of the upper 20 percent remained constant at about 41 percent. Other sectors likewise showed only minor changes.

Various studies, including one by the Census Bureau itself, suggest the official figures on income shares reflect a gross understatement of the downward transfer of income. This will be discussed later. At the moment, we are concerned with the effectiveness of the private system in distributing income. Looking at it from this view, the picture is far less static than it might appear.

For one thing, the same people move up and down the scale as they advance through life. Bureau of the Census data shows that the median income of families with a householder

FIGURE 3-3. Percentage Share of Aggregate Income by Fifths of Families

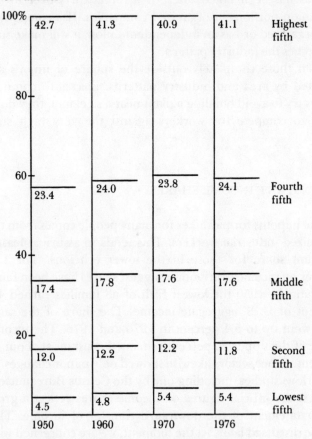

Source: Department of Commerce, Bureau of the Census.

between 14 and 24 years of age was $9,440 in 1976. In the 45- to 54-year-old age bracket, the median income was over $19,000. For those over 65, the median dropped to $8,720. There is no question that age factors exaggerate the imbalance of the income structure. A young doctor makes less than an old doctor, but their lifetime incomes may be the same.

That still leaves the problem of why the top 5 percent of all families should receive over ten times more income than families in the lowest 5 percent. Harvard's John Rawls states that incomes and other values are to be distributed equally "unless an unequal distribution of any, or all, of these values is to everybody's advantage." Rawls is emphatic that the poorest people must be among those benefiting from any income redistribution.

It would seem to follow that inequality should be considered good if it is more advantageous to poor people than the only alternative. That does seem to be the case with the American system. As will be shown, the greatest progress for the poorest people has come when the system operated with the least government intrusion.

LARGER INCOME SIZE

What has happened is that the constant shares of income have produced larger incomes at all levels. In 1976, figure 3–4 shows, the upper limit of income for families in the lowest 20 percent was $7,441. In 1950, the lowest 20 percent of families had incomes under $1,700 (in 1950 dollars).

The goodness of the American system shows up in the rising levels of income for all people. A Conference Board article by Gabian Linden ("The Classes: Upward," *Across the Board*, April 1977) examined this change primarily from the viewpoint of identifying markets. "The rise of family earnings has transformed the consumer market in a comparatively brief time," wrote Linden. "For instance, in 1955, half the total personal income accrued to families with annual earnings in excess of $11,000. Ten years later the cutoff point had moved up to $15,000 and it now exceeds $20,000" (in 1975 dollars).

Corresponding to this increase in income has been a reduction of the lower-income population. In the mid-Fifties,

FIGURE 3-4. Family Income Levels by Fifths of Families (upper limits of fifths in current dollars)

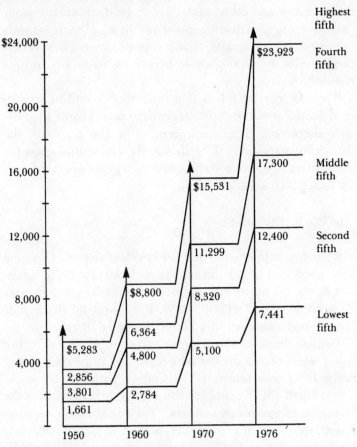

Source: Department of Commerce, Bureau of the Census.

about 25 million, or 60 percent of all families, had annual incomes of less than $10,000 (in today's prices). These families accounted for approximately 35 percent of total buying power. "But," says Linden, "over the years, the importance of this group shrivels appreciably. By the mid-Seventies, it constituted less than 20 million or under 35 percent of all homes . . . . Thus, in a mere two decades, what had once

FIGURE 3-5. Percent Distribution of Families and Aggregate Income by Income Class (based on 1975 dollars)

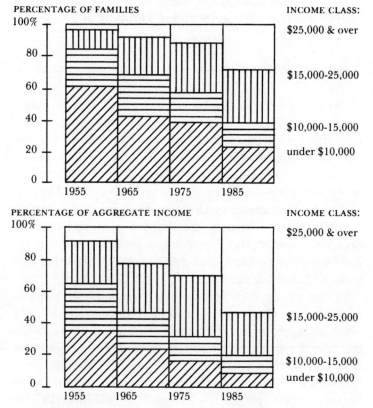

Source: Fabian Linden, "The Classes: Upward," *Across the Board* (April 1977). Courtesy of The Conference Board.

been the nation's mass market has contracted to a relatively minor segment."

The pattern of more affluence and less penury holds true at all levels. Families in the $15,000-to-$25,000 income bracket, measured in 1975 dollars, went from 13 percent of the total in 1950 to 30 percent in the mid-Seventies. These numbers actually understate the gain, because the percentage of younger families in the bracket was nearly double that of 10 years earlier. These families—30 percent of the total— were still well below the earning peaks. In short, there has been a dramatic upward movement of people's income. This has resulted from constant shares of a growing pie.

THE POVERTY BRACKET

The general rise in standard of living has left some people behind. In 1977, over 9 percent of all families and unrelated individuals were classed as poverty-stricken. (The 1976 poverty cutoff ranged from just under $2,800 for a single person to over $9,500 for a family of seven.) But looked at collectively, the poor *did* share in the general uplift. The 9.4-percent poverty group in 1977 was down from 18.5 percent in 1959. On the basis of the Rawls dictum and common decency, however, this improvement isn't enough. It is not good for some people to be living in luxury while others are going without basic necessities.

So the system isn't perfect, but it seems to be the best available. The alternative showed up to some extent in 1975, when a deep recession brought a shrinkage of the economic pie. Social spending rose but poverty increased. Transfer payments increased to $176 billion in 1975, up $36 billion from 1974. With the pie shrinking, however, the number of poverty-stricken people rose, from 23.3 million in 1974 to

25.9 million in 1975. The percentage of people in poverty rose from 8.8 percent in 1974 to 9.7 percent in 1975.

It would be stretching a point to say government redistribution caused the 1975 rise in poverty. The recession—brought on by the oil shock, general inflation, and other factors—caused the rise. On the other hand, it's interesting to speculate what would have happened if the government had cut taxes by $36 billion at the start of 1975 instead of boosting social spending by that amount.

Recent history suggests the tax cut would have been more effective than the spending rise in reducing poverty. In the first half of the Sixties, the Kennedy administration cut taxes. This produced exuberant growth. In the second half of the Sixties, tax policies of the Johnson and Nixon administrations were generally repressive. The growth rate was cut in half. At about the same time, social spending zoomed. Transfer payments went from $44.7 billion in 1966 to over $94 billion in 1971. That compared with an increase of about $18 billion from 1959 to 1966.

According to table 3–1, in the earlier period of 1959–66, the number of people in the poverty bracket declined by nearly eleven million. From 1966 to 1971, the number in poverty fell by only about three million.

The poverty statistics aren't ironclad, and by picking the right years, it's possible to get varied results. Nevertheless, it stands to reason that the greatest benefit is going to come from policies that promote high employment rates rather than policies designed to make unemployment bearable.

In the sequence of the Sixties, social spending contributed to tax policies that eventually brought the economy to a standstill and created high unemployment. In the years before social spending became so massive, there was some evidence that income shares as well as income levels in the lowest brackets benefited from good times. And vice versa—

larger incomes in the lowest brackets encourage a healthy
economy. The income share of the lowest fifth dipped in the
1954 recession and rose in the 1955 boom. There was another
dip in the sluggish years before the Kennedy administration.

AFFLUENCE FOR ALL

At the most, income redistribution will merely lift poor
people to survival levels. That isn't good enough. The aim
should be to make everyone well-to-do. This can be done if

TABLE 3-1. Persons Below the Poverty Level

YEAR	NUMBER (IN THOUSANDS)	POVERTY RATE (PERCENTAGE OF ALL PERSONS)
1959	39,490	22.4
1960	39,851	22.2
1961	39,628	21.9
1962	38,625	21.0
1963	36,436	19.5
1964	36,055	19.0
1965	33,185	17.3
1966	30,424	15.7
1967	27,769	14.2
1968	25,389	12.8
1969	24,147	12.1
1970	25,420	12.6
1971	25,559	12.5
1972	24,460	11.9
1973	22,973	11.1
1974	23,370	11.2
1975	25,877	12.3
1976	24,975	11.8

Source: Department of Commerce, Bureau of the Census.

poor people are put to work and enough wealth is created.

Given a chance, the American system will elevate people's standard of living. This has been happening on a collective basis. It is happening on an individual basis. According to the Internal Revenue Service, the number of millionaires in the country rose from 60,000 in 1962 to 180,000 in 1972. Just by looking at the names of industry leaders, you can see the movement of people from an immigrant's poverty to the top of the heap. Irving Shapiro was chairman of DuPont in 1978; Tom Murphy was head of General Motors; Lee Iacocca had been a top dog at Ford until his run-in with Henry Ford. Of recent presidents, Lyndon Johnson and Richard Nixon rose from modest circumstances, if not poverty; John Kennedy was a generation or so removed from an Irish immigrant's status; Harry Truman came back after bankruptcy as a retailer. William Roesch, executive vice president of United States Steel Corporation, started as a clerk in a coal mining operation. Roesch got his engineering degree by going to college at night for twelve years. J. Willard Marriott started with a root beer stand in Washington, D. C., and ended up with a chain of hotels. These are just a few conspicuous examples. Look around at the successful people you know and see how many started out from near the poverty level.

People's desire to do their own spending was most strongly reflected in June of 1978, when 4.2 million Californians voted themselves a two-thirds reduction in property taxes. The people of the state were voting to keep more of their earned incomes. They were also voting against government taking more control over the disbursal of income. Most voters figured they were doing better under the private system of uneven distribution than under a system in which government tried to redistribute large portions of their earnings.

Chapter 4

PROGRESS AND ECONOMIC REWARDS

New York Republican Congressman Jack Kemp, business leaders, and others feel the free market is being stifled by heavy taxation. It's argued that innovation, effort, and risk-taking are all being discouraged because taxes are reducing the rewards for success. At the same time, there are those who believe there should be a further reduction in the rewards. According to this school, a greater income transfer would have an equalizing effect without significant economic losses.

These conflicting opinions raise questions as to the nature of progress. With today's computers and automatic machines, is effort really that important? Given that there is still a need to innovate and work hard, should there not be a tighter limit on the rewards for success?

The answer to the first question is, yes, effort is important. Progress has never come easy, even to the most gifted people: Gail Borden suffered a series of devastating setbacks before he succeeded in the milk buisness; Rowland Macy had three dry goods stores go sour before he found the right combination in New York. With all today's technology, progress is not automatic. Some technologically advanced nations are standing still or going downhill. Progress results from strenuous effort, difficult decisions, and dangerous risks.

And yes, although it's important that there be rewards for those who succeed, there should be limits—and the free process does provide these. If a company is too greedy, competitors will take away business; if management is too stingy, human nature being what it is, workers will refuse to work—no one can hoard success.

THE 1960s: THE SYSTEM AT WORK

At the end of the 1960s, I set out to trace the workings of economic progress over the previous decade. This was a period of almost uninterrupted growth and prosperity. National output increased 79 percent, while productivity and real income rose more than 30 percent. The Sixties showed how the U. S. system can perform when given a reasonable chance. A look back at some of the events that produced so much progress seems worthwhile.

The Aluminum Can Industry
One example was the push of aluminum companies into the container market. Prior to this, aluminum had been made on a job-shop basis. Small specialized orders were processed in small, slow mills. To put the operation on a volume basis, the aluminum companies needed an application that took large quantities of standard material.

The can market was the perfect answer to this need. Accordingly, aluminum producers invented easy-open ends and new drawing techniques. The price of aluminum container sheet was set a few cents above the raw ingot. Scrap recycling systems were set up. Marketing programs were launched. The aluminum people were rewarded for these efforts. They captured over half the beer and soft drink market. This success came at the expense of steel producers, who once had had the can market to themselves.

Steel mills reacted by finding ways to produce can stock in much thinner gauges: the mills spent $180 million on thin tinplate and later another $40 million on tin-free steel, reducing the weight of the average can a third. With a competitive battle on their hands, steel people passed along a good part of the savings.

"There has never been a period in my time when we have not had substantial discipline working on us," said George Stinson, chairman of National Steel Corporation. The discipline was such that three steel companies dropped out of the container market. With tough pricing and reduced weight, the material cost of a steel can dropped 12 percent in the Sixties.

While sharing their progress with customers, the steel companies were also sharing with employees. The freedom of people to work or not work forced steel companies to grant increases that raised employment costs 46 percent in the Sixties.

The aluminum companies were likewise sharing. Straight-time earnings of aluminum workers went from $2.63 an hour in 1960 to $3.70 in 1970. The net increase in aluminum prices was 3¢ a pound, from 26¢ in 1960 to 29¢ in 1970.

The can companies were in no position to hoard or ignore progress. To justify its existence, explained William Woodside of American Can Company, a can company had to show it could do a better job of making containers than could food or beverage companies. The more new developments the company could produce, the more they protected and fostered their business. Accordingly, the can companies tooled up rapidly for thin tinplate and aluminum ends. New seams were developed to permit the use of tin-free steel.

While they were doing these things, the can companies were also souping up line speeds. "Ten years ago you would talk 300 to 350 cans a minute," said Woodside. "We're now running 500 to 600 a minute. We're talking about lines that will have speeds of 1200 a minute."

The Sheet Metal Industry

The kind of mass production characteristic of today's can and container industry requires a metal sheet that is smooth and uniform. In the late Fifties National Steel built a giant hot strip mill with twice the muscle and speed of anything then running. It was highly automated.

There is always a risk when equipment is scaled up. And a hot strip mill is as complicated as any machine in industry. It consists of up to eleven separate rolling stands in tandem. Steel slabs heated to over 2000° F flow continuously through the stands at speeds of more than 3,000 feet per minute. In scaling up speeds, sizes, and power inputs, National Steel was risking a disastrous failure. Moreover, the company made its decision in the middle of a steel slump. This made it possible to buy equipment at bargain prices, but it meant National Steel would have to eat a lot of steel if there was no recovery.

The market did recover and after considerable debugging, the mill did work. The new facility enabled National Steel to supply large coils rolled to close tolerances. The company began advertising that customers could get more fenders and more refrigerator doors out of a ton of its steel than a ton of competitors' steel.

Shortly after that everyone began putting in new strip mills. When these were on stream, enterprising salesmen quietly advised customers they could have sheet rolled to half the commercial tolerance. The mills wound up eliminating all tolerances for price purposes. If a sheet was heavier than the specified thickness, the customer did not pay for the extra weight.

Involved in all this is a difficult, process of individual and corporate risk-taking. "We sweated blood," said Lewis W. Foy, chairman of Bethlehem Steel Corporation. He was recalling Bethlehem's decision to spend $1 billion on a complete new plant at Burns Harbor, Indiana. The risk did pay off. Burns Harbor is Bethlehem's high-profit, low-cost mill. It has given the company a production base in the big midwestern market. Without the prospect of reward, Bethlehem would not have put $1 billion into an investment that would offer no return for four or five years.

The Appliance Industry

One of the truly remarkable stories of the Sixties was in the appliance industry. At General Electric's Appliance Park in Louisville, Kentucky, straight-time pay increased 35 percent from 1960 to 1970. In this period, the price of the average appliance fell 16 percent.

As the price decline suggests, appliance people were able to make enormous efficiency gains in the Sixties. This was done by installing highly automated mass-production lines. As the price drop also suggests, automation promotes competition. To keep their high-speed lines running, the appliance companies needed volume. Attempts to get volume sales forced prices down, and the price decline brought pressure for further automation as a means of lowering costs.

Competition also fostered product innovation. General Electric worked seven years to develop a self-cleaning oven. "There were risks all along," said appliance and television group vice president Stanley Gault, but the company persisted. "There is extreme competition. We are the leader. We knew there was a very desirable benefit." Aside from financial gain, he saw as another form of progress the "upgrading" of people. Although mechanization is frequently blamed for reducing work to a dull, repetitive chore, Gault isn't sure all workers want challenging jobs. At Appliance Park, he feels, many workers prefer to reserve a good part of their energy for farming and other outside activities; automation allows this reserve of energy.

In any case, automation is now reaching the point where operators are replaced by engineers and technicians. By 1970, Gulf Oil Corporation had 22,000 salaried people compared to 11,000 hourly workers. "You can walk through refineries and see very few people," said Zane Q. Johnson, executive vice president at that time. The elevation of people at Gulf resulted from an investment increase from $45,000 per worker in 1960 to $75,000 in 1970. What happens to the people you don't see? It may take a generation or so, but many of them have moved up with the process. Zane Johnson's father was a driller in the oil fields. The son became an executive vice president. "The American dream is not a farce if you're willing to work," said Johnson. "You've got to have a little luck, too," he added.

The Farming Industry

The farming industry is America's great success story. One reason it was possible to have guns and butter during the Vietnam War was that the million-man increase in the armed services was matched by a million-man reduction in the people needed for farming during the Sixties (see figure 4–1).

"No one knows how much the American farmer can produce," said Mel Curvey, product manager for International Harvester. "There has never been a full test of the farmer's ability to produce." Curvey cited a case where one man with modern tools was operating a 700-acre farm. But the equipment people deny they have mechanized the family farm out of existence. As of 1970, more than 90 percent of all farms were still in the family class. They had fewer than two hired hands. It is true, however, that a large portion of total output is coming from a small percentage of all farms.

As to why the Soviet collectives have never matched the American performance, economist LaVon Fife of International Harvester expressed what he called a "personal bias." "My feeling is that there are satisfactions and motivations peculiar to agriculture that arise out of ownership and seeing the things grow."

THE INCENTIVE TO PROGRESS

The march of progress involves constant pushing and shoving. Some years ago, Amsted Industries, Incorporated was being pushed out of the market for freight car wheels. The market was being taken over by wrought steel. "The demise of the chilled iron wheel was definite," said Joseph P. Lanterman, then chairman of Amsted.

FIGURE 4-1. Farm and Military Employment—1960-1969 (in thousands)

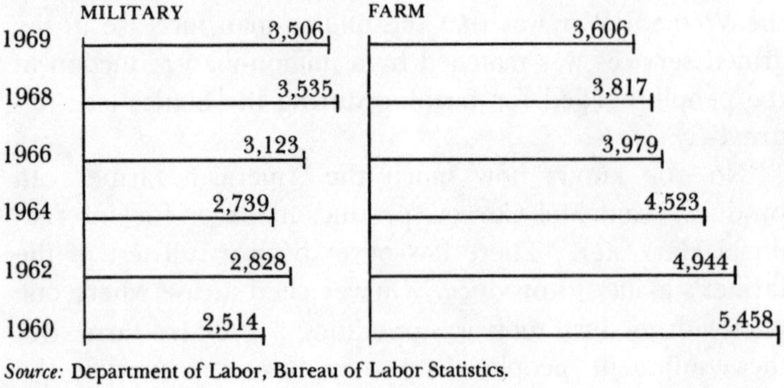

	MILITARY	FARM
1969	3,506	3,606
1968	3,535	3,817
1966	3,123	3,979
1964	2,739	4,523
1962	2,828	4,944
1960	2,514	5,458

Source: Department of Labor, Bureau of Labor Statistics.

Rather than join the horse and buggy, Amsted rushed development of its pressure pouring process. Betting heavily on the soundness of the new method, the company skipped the pilot stage and built two production plants. When these were operating, the new product was put on the market at a low price. Amsted subsequently achieved price parity along with a third of the market.

Brisk competition persisted, however. Steel wheel prices rose only 10 percent in the Sixties. Base wages at Amsted rose 50 percent. "The incentive to take the risk was the disappearance of profits," explained Lanterman. Having built a superior mousetrap, Amsted was rewarded handsomely.

The growth experienced by Amsted and other companies doesn't just happen on its own. Progress is not an automatic, push-button occurrence—there must be vigorous striving for fame and fortune. People must be able to hope for the best. There must be the means and the incentive to work hard and well.

If the right ingredients aren't present, a country can decline. Civilizations *have* gone down and disappeared. The problems of Great Britain and the failure of the Soviet Union are warnings that modern technology is not a guarantee against decay.

In our country, we have seen the railroad system shrink and deteriorate. If Bethlehem Steel were facing its Burns Harbor decisions today, the company would probably take its billion dollars and put it in savings bonds. There is a growing disinclination to risk money or extend effort. Says Congressman Jack Kemp, "Millions of Americans are sheltering income, . . . millions of low-income people are prevented from taking jobs because the after-tax gains of becoming employed do not offset the concurrent loss in social services, . . . millions of workers would work harder and more productively at lower tax rates."

High tax rates in the United States are related directly to excessive government spending—particularly social spending. And there is no question that high levels of social spending in the socialist countries have been accompanied by economic disaster.

THE SWEDISH EXCEPTION

Until recently, Sweden was regarded as the one big exception to this rule. In chapter 2 a study by the Federal Reserve Bank of St. Louis was cited that showed that on the basis of actual purchasing power, Sweden's per-capita GNP is still well below that of the United States (see figure 2–3). Nevertheless, Sweden did seem to be doing quite well with a highly socialized economy. Arthur Okun discussed this point in jocular tones at a Washington meeting on income redistribution sponsored by the American Enterprise Institute for Public Policy Research: "Once before on a panel of this sort, I made a nonaggression pact with a conservative member of the panel. If he refrained from saying anything about the United Kingdom, I would refrain from mentioning Sweden."

This was a pretty good bargain for the conservative. It left him with the whole pattern of socialist failure in Eastern Europe, the Soviet Union, East Germany, and North Korea. Sweden is the only exception. Why?

It can be argued that the "particular talents" of the Swedes have produced a measure of prosperity in spite of the system. And this might be defensible, as it's probable, although not certain, for instance, that Japan would be a prosperous country under *any* system. The Japanese seem to have a "special aptitude" for industrialization.

A second point is that more than 90 percent of Sweden's industry is privately owned. And while Sweden is socialistic in the treatment of personal income, it is more capitalistic than the United States in the treatment of business. Corporate income tax rates are about the same in the two countries, but Sweden allows more liberal depreciation. Up to 40 percent of a Swedish company's profit can be exempted from taxes if earmarked for investment. No corporate tax is paid on dividends remitted by the foreign subsidiaries of Swedish companies.

But there are signs that Sweden's prosperity is coming to an end. A part of this prosperity came from the sale of raw materials. "As recently as 1969, we were the leading iron ore exporters in the world," said Benjt Lovkvist, director of the Kiruna ore pelletizing plant. In 1969, Sweden was exporting thirty million tons of ore while Brazil was selling twenty million tons. In 1977, Brazil exported 73 million tons and Sweden only 21 million. Whereas Sweden must dig deeper for its iron, Brazil has easily accessible deposits. The low cost of Brazilian ore is forcing Sweden to sell at a loss. In 1978 the Kiruna complex was losing $400,000 a day.

If socialism should not be blamed for the depletion of ore reserves, it should not be credited with the prosperity that came from these reserves.

An October, 1977, study by the Conference Board suggests Sweden is losing ground rather than pulling ahead. Dealing with the salaries of engineers, the study compared the amount of work time required in different countries to buy consumer goods and services. "In Sweden, hours of work required went up sharply by about 20 percent [from 1971 to 1975]. . . . Whereas consumer prices rose by 37 percent, salaries in Kroner increased by only 23 percent between 1971 and 1975. In no country was the relative movement of prices and salaries so adverse to the increase in real income."

There are those who feel this kind of change is not accidental. They see socialism having an enervating effect.

Writing in the *New York Times* (Nov. 11, 1977), Leonard Silk had this report: "An outstanding Swedish economist, Professor Assar Lindbeck of the University of Stockholm, who is a Social Democrat, believes that the real causes of the 'Swedish sickness' are those against which Professor Friedrich Haydek had warned during the Depression: that the welfare state, with its burgeoning social benefits and high taxation, would in the end arrest the dynamism of the economic system. But he does not think the threat is to democracy, as did Professor Haydek, but to the pluralism of the society on which an effective economic performance rests. Professor Lindbeck sees Swedish companies losing their innovativeness."

The Swedes are still very inventive. Every other day, they seem to come up with some new process for making steel. However, it appears that state involvement is steering innovation away from practical reality.

One big university group was commissioned to devise a plan for making the Swedish steel industry more efficient. The ultimate phase of the plan calls for all steel to be made in plasma furnaces. This makes fascinating reading, but it isn't likely to help the Swedish steel industry in the next twenty or thirty years. Meanwhile, the Japanese have twenty or thirty engineers with clipboards probing into blast furnaces, figuring how to get a few more tons an hour.

A LESSON FROM GREAT BRITAIN

England's troubles are dealt with in the book *Britain's Economic Problem: Too Few Producers* by Oxford economists Robert Bacon and Walter Eltis (New York: St. Martin's Press, 1978). As the title suggests, Britain is in a situation in which too few people are turning out goods and too many have gone into government. The authors document their point very clearly. In earlier years Britain went through a vigorous modernization program. "By 1971," said the authors, "the service life and average age of British machine tools were almost exactly the same as in the U.S.A. over a very wide range of machine tool categories and user industries."

Reflecting this, industrial productivity in Britain rose 4 percent a year from 1965 to 1974. At about the same time, however, government social services and taxes were increasing. This brought demands from workers for pay increases to preserve or increase take-home pay. These demands brought inflation and government measures to curb inflation. Because of the measures or the inflation, there wasn't enough demand to soak up the goods available from added productivity. "Industrial production increased less than half as fast as productivity with the result that more than half the benefits from extra productivity resulted not in the production of more goods, but in employment of fewer men for shorter hours."

One consequence of the inflationary curbs and reduced demand was a shift of workers from industrial to government employment. This added to the tax drag. It reduced national productivity by moving people into nonproductive work. A second consequence was resistance by workers to anything that would increase their efficiency and thereby endanger their jobs. With roughly the same tools, wrote the authors, "each American worker produced two and three times as much as each British worker."

A crucial factor in Britain has unquestionably been the diversion of money and men into the machinery of government. The authors warn that this same process is at work in the United States and Canada. "Like Britain, also, their nonmarket spending has risen very rapidly. The result has been that all three countries have diverted a high fraction of the extra resources resulting from economic growth to their nonmarket sectors, leaving relatively little for their market sectors where all marketed output is produced."

THE SOVIET UNION

If people do not receive, in perceptible rewards, what they feel are their just desserts, it stands to reason that they will drag their feet. Reports from the Soviet Union underscore this truth: "Many people are unwilling to put in a day's work," wrote *Time* (March, 1976). "A recent study, based on Soviet statistics, showed that each day 1 million people out of an industrial work force of 84 million do not turn up for work."

This performance is not surprising. "All classes have experienced repression during sixty years of Communist rule," wrote Valery Chalidze in the *Wall Street Journal* (May 16, 1978). "The overwhelming majority of Soviet workers live in poverty." Chalidze cited a letter from Leonid Sery, an Odessa worker, to George Meany. "As Soviet workers, we are not even entitled to ask for a raise. Our only right is to work, receiving miserly wages bearing no relation to our family's needs."

The trouble with socialism is that it neglects the flawed state of human nature. If we were more perfect beings, we would be happy to work hard and share out output with less productive neighbors. As it is, a system can succeed only if it gives play to the baser qualities in our natures. "Every sustained wave of technological progress and economic development everywhere has been fueled by greed, profiteering, special privileges, and megalomania," wrote Theodore Levitt, professor of business administration at Harvard. Instead of focusing on the negative business of closing tax loopholes, Levitt indicates, government should bring the "dark side" of man to bear on problems.

In dealing with the energy shortage, he says, there should be "almost irresponsibly massive infusions of money." We may lament this fact, but money does seem to be the root of all progress. The reason, again, is that progress doesn't come easily. We have lighter beer cans because numerous individuals staked their careers on the feasibility of using lighter materials. There must be the prospect of reward for this kind of risk to be taken.

The system must recognize our failings, but it must also work to curb them. Competition in a free system provides a means of policing the process. This is a far more effective check on avarice than any form of regulation. Apart from the question of effort, the enormously complex business of delivering the right product to the right place at the right time requires a multitude of decisions. In Russia, where the state controls distribution, stores wind up with toothbrushes and no toothpaste. In the United States, where companies respond to the free market, there is an amazingly precise meshing of supply and demand.

The system works. It is superior to any system yet devised.

Chapter 5

GOVERNMENT POLICY AND CAPITAL FORMATION

In the middle of the last century, Andrew Carnegie commuted by train between his office in downtown Pittsburgh and his home in the east end of the city. You can't do that any more. A century of progress has left Pittsburgh with practically no rail service despite an extensive network of track. Today, even traveling to the city by bus or car is a problem, because half the bridges are falling down. This is just a conspicuous example of deterioration in the nation's capital infrastructure and industrial base. At best, we have been moving ahead more slowly—and in a number of key areas, we have been falling back.

There is an urgent need to rebuild and modernize. We have a lot of catching up to do. At the same time, there are extraordinary needs in the future. The energy program alone will require almost as much investment in the next ten years as went into all capital projects in the last ten.

OUR DETERIORATING CAPITAL BASE

As to what's wrong and what's needed, business has an uncomplicated answer. Too much of the nation's output is being commandeered by government. Through taxation of individuals and corporations, government has removed income from the sources of investment dollars. The dollars have been transferred downward to individuals who put most of their incomes into immediate consumption. As business sees it, there must be tax relief for corporations and for individuals who save. At the same time, government spending must be curbed. The transfer of income from savers to consumers must be checked.

As evidence of the capital lag, business cites more rapid rates of progress abroad. From 1960 to 1973, productivity rose 10.7 percent a year in Japan. That compared with a U. S. gain of 3.3 percent a year. (The most recent period has been even worse.) Even the much-maligned British economy advanced more rapidly than that of the United States from 1960 to 1973. All the major industrial nations did better than the United States.

Closely related is the fact that all major nations have been ploughing more of their output back into capital improvements (see figure 5–1). From 1960 to 1973, Japan's spending came to 35 percent of Gross National Product (GNP). The U. S. figure was 18 percent.

These numbers strongly suggest that the United States is falling behind because it is not spending enough. But in 1975 congressional testimony, Joseph Pechman of Brookings Institution offered a different interpretation. It was not so much a case of our falling behind as of others catching up, Pechman argued. Larger capital inputs were to be expected in the less mature foreign economies.

There is some truth to this statement. It is also true that the destruction during World War II created a special need to rebuild in Germany and Japan. However, the war ended 35 years ago. It is becoming less reasonable that more rapid progress abroad can be explained on the basis of catching up. At least one foreign nation, Japan, is now moving past us in many areas.

FIGURE 5-1. Capital Investment and Productivity

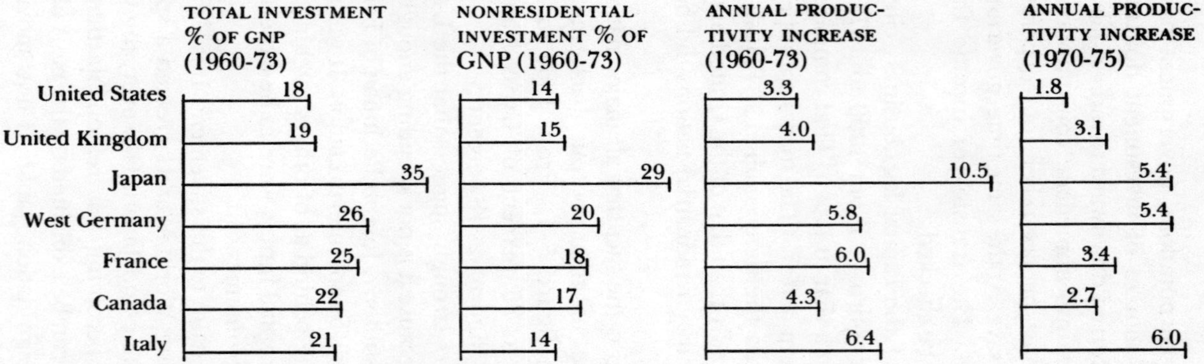

	TOTAL INVESTMENT % OF GNP (1960-73)	NONRESIDENTIAL INVESTMENT % OF GNP (1960-73)	ANNUAL PRODUC-TIVITY INCREASE (1960-73)	ANNUAL PRODUC-TIVITY INCREASE (1970-75)
United States	18	14	3.3	1.8
United Kingdom	19	15	4.0	3.1
Japan	35	29	10.5	5.4
West Germany	26	20	5.8	5.4
France	25	18	6.0	3.4
Canada	22	17	4.3	2.7
Italy	21	14	6.4	6.0

Source: Business Roundtable, May 1975; Bureau of Labor Statistics.

In determining the exact state of affairs, the difficulty is that international productivity statistics deal almost entirely with changes, not levels. There are, however, complete figures on steel. These show that Japan's amazing productivity gains were partly a reflection of a low starting level. In 1964 output per man-hour of Japanese steel mills was only about half that of U. S. mills. But, as has been indicated, Japan has done more than catch up. The Japanese boosted steel productivity 166 percent between 1964 and 1975. They have developed the most modern steel industry in the world.

With a higher starting level, the American steel industry had less room for improvement. Even so, the U. S. gain was substandard: 17 percent, or 1.9 percent a year from 1964 to 1975.

LAGGING PRODUCTIVITY

American productivity is not just lagging in relation to other nations. The rate of progress is down from our own past record. From 1950 to 1970, U. S. output per man-hour rose 2.5 percent a year. From 1970 through 1977, the increase was 1.5 percent a year. Productivity rose only 0.4 pct in 1978.

Whatever the cause, there is no question about the effect of the lag. "Were it not for the productivity slowdown, today's gross national output would be $220 billion larger," said Reginald Jones of General Electric in 1977, "and in the past ten years, we would have produced nearly a trillion dollars more in goods and services."

Various factors have been at work, but the slowdown has been partly due to a shortage of capital. This was clearly indicated in 1973 and 1974 when unemployment remained high despite booming demand. The 4.8-percent jobless rate in 1973 compared with 3.4 percent in 1968, another year of peak demand. There wasn't just an imbalance of supply and demand in 1973; there was an imbalance of men and machines.

The object lesson of 1973 and 1974 did not bring serious consideration of tax remedies until 1975. By then, there was a recession. Plant utilization fell to 68 percent of capacity, the lowest level since the Depression of the Thirties. It was difficult to argue the nation was being held back by a shortage of capital and capacity. "A much more serious constraint on investment than the tax system is the recession," Joseph Pechman told Congress in June of 1975.

It was certainly true that capital spending was held down in 1975 partly because existing plants were sitting idle. Business people tried to show that the shortages of 1974 brought on the recession of 1975 with its low operating rates. When the economy returned to normal, business warned, there would again be shortages of goods and capacity. The long-term problem of capital formation should not be dealt with on the basis of short-term fluctuations of the economy, company officials contended.

None of these arguments had much effect. As has been said, the capital formation crusade of 1975 flopped. The economy was simply not short of capital at the time legislation was being considered. There was a recession. It's worth noting that the capital spending lag was a cause as well as an effect of the 1975 recession. The recession was not the result of reduced consumer outlays because personal spending rose 10 percent in 1975. Even after deducting 7 percent world of inflation, real spending was higher in 1975 than in 1974. On the other hand, there was a 6-percent or 7-percent decrease in capital spending in 1975 after adjusting for inflation.

Much more clear-cut was the manner in which a sluggish capital upturn slowed the recovery from the 1975 recession.

Capital spending normally trails consumer spending, but in the 1975 cycle, as figure 5–2 shows, the lag time was abnormally long. By early 1978, the capital rise was still far slower than in past cycles. "Since reaching a cyclical low point in late 1975," reported the Mellon Bank of Pittsburgh in May of 1978, "construction contracts for new manufacturing plants, as measured in square feet, have climbed a very modest 28 percent, a dismal showing as compared with the 87-percent increase recorded during the 1970–73 expansion." In the second half of 1978 there was still no surge in the building of steel mills, paper plants, power stations, or oil refineries. The structural fabricators, who depend on this kind of activity, were starving to death.

The capital lag helps explain why unemployment averaged over 7 percent in both 1976 and 1977. Capital spending is often thought of only in terms or providing tools for future jobs, but there is also immediate job creation as the tools and plants are built. This immediate effect plays an essential role

FIGURE 5-2. Business Expenditures for New Plant and Equipment (in billions of dollars)

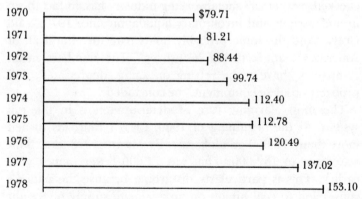

Year	Expenditure
1970	$79.71
1971	81.21
1972	88.44
1973	99.74
1974	112.40
1975	112.78
1976	120.49
1977	137.02
1978	153.10

Source: Department of Commerce.

in bringing the economy to full prosperity. And because of its long-term nature, capital spending serves to bridge the gaps between consumer spending dips. In both respects, there was a capital deficiency in the 1975–78 cycle.

INDUSTRIAL OBSOLESCENCE

According to the National Machine Tool Builders Association (NMTBA), the most recent lag was part of a long trend. In arriving at this conclusion, the association studied sixteen metalworking companies. Records of the companies were checked first, and it was found they were representative of the whole durable goods industry. On the basis of its sample, NMTBA reported a deterioration of the plant and equipment base over the last thirteen years (figure 5–3). "Real capital spending has been declining and declining rather steadily since 1965," said James Gray, president of the association.

The decline is even worse than it appears, said Gray, because much of the spending in recent years has been for nonproductive environmental equipment. NMTBA reported a sharp reduction in the real asset value of companies checked. "America's metalworking industry has, in fact, been in unconscious and involuntary liquidation since 1970," said Gray. "And the same probably holds true for almost all of America's manufacturing industries." The numbers mean companies "have to be relying on aging, depreciated, and probably obsolete equipment," he concluded.

The most alarming case of deterioration is in the rail system. At the beginning of 1969, Class I railroads owned more than 176,000 gondola cars. By May of 1978, the count was down to 132,000. That was 11,000 fewer than a year earlier. This is particularly disturbing because the nation's conversion to coal hinges on an adequate supply of freight cars. "The more I hear about the railroads, the more I worry," said T. J. Whyte, executive vice president, Consolidation Coal. To make matters worse, the capability for rebuilding railroads has been eroded. The last U. S. rail mill was built in 1920. One of the few mills still operating dates back to 1902.

The overall steel situation is hardly encouraging. Bethlehem Steel Corporation in 1977 shut down portions of its plants in Johnstown, Pennsylvania, and Lackawanna, New York. Alan Wood Steel Corporation went bankrupt. Youngstown Sheet & Tube Company closed most of its Campbell Works. All told, more than four million tons of steel capacity were scrapped in 1977, as mills were too ancient to

FIGURE 5-3. Book Value of Fixed Assets of 16 Metalworking Companies

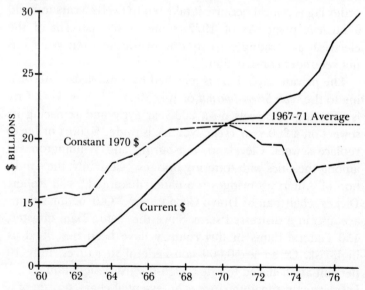

Sources: Department of Commerce; National Machine Tool Builders Association.
Courtesy of National Machine Tool Builders Assoc.

survive in the highly competitive 1977 market. There are predictions that another 15 percent of the nation's steel capacity will have to be retired at a time when we already have to import steel to meet our needs.

There are other areas where extreme obsolescence will make itself felt. For example there were only fifteen new power plants ordered in 1977. "Normally, there should be fifty power plants ordered a year," said R. E. Reardon, manager of energy analysis for Westinghouse Electric Corporation. Despite all the fussing about energy, our dependence on foreign oil is increasing. The trend toward increased use of imported oil was briefly checked in 1978, but our long-term position is worsening.

The 1977 orders for power plants included a grand total of two nuclear plants. As of 1978, there had been no net addition to the backlogs of nuclear suppliers since 1974. The order lag is critical because it take ten to twelve years to build a nuclear plant. As of 1977, some twenty percent of the electrical generating capacity due in the next ten years was not yet under construction.

The private capital lag is matched by a public lag. According to the *Wall Street Journal* of July 20, 1978, New York City is repaving its streets on a 200-year cycle and replacing its sewers on a 300-year cycle. Newark is under a court order to replace sewers. Cleveland, Pittsburgh, and Wilmington are among the cities with tottering bridges. "Certainly, the condition of America's bridges is a national scandal," said Robert Dickey, chairman of Dravo Corporation. "Our nation's dams are also in a distressed state. Since the Teton Dam disaster, 150 Federal dams in this country have been described as high-risk. Of some 50,000 non-Federal structures, fully 10 percent are believed to rate a high-hazard designation . . . . Infrastructure maintenance is an essential characteristic of a developed nation."

It may seem inconsistent to complain about government spending and at the same time talk about the need to shore up public structures. Business people have been known to reverse their fields when the spending involves their own products. However, there are capital needs in the public sector. Like those of corporations, government's capital outlays have been squeezed by social spending.

THE COMING CRUNCH

Whether we are behind or ahead, there are extraordinary needs in the future. The coal industry produced 688 million tons in 1977. The government's energy program called for 1.2 billion tons of coal by 1985. It will take an estimated $22 billion to reach the target. That same amount was to be spend by the electrical industry in just one year, 1978. "In terms of capacity additions, the estimate for the 1978–82 period is 110,000 megawatts," said Karl H. Rudolph, chairman of the Cleveland Electric Illuminating Company. With no adjustment for inflation, this addition will cost $135 billion.

Requirements of the whole energy field are huge. James E. Lee, president of Gulf Oil Corporation, gave this rundown of things that need to be done: find oil at the rate of a new Alaskan North Slope every three years, add 12 percent to the coal supply, finish three times as much nuclear power potential as we have constructed. "The cost of doing all this by 1985 will be in the order of hundreds of billions of dollars," said Lee. "Perhaps in excess of one trillion."

The capital requirement of the railroads is placed at $5.3 billion a year. The yearly figure is $2.8 billion more than the railroads spent in 1977.

The steel industry is projecting a need for another thrity million tons of capacity by 1985. With replacement and

environmental costs thrown in, the total capital requirement
is enormous. "We find an annual need for $6.22 billion, or
the staggering total of nearly $50 billion by 1985," said Harry
Holiday, president of Armco Inc. In 1977, the steel industry
spent less than $3 billion.

Pollution abatement has created a special new need for
capital: $217 billion for the ten years ending in 1983. There
must be a larger investment in research. "If we look at U. S.
effort in comparison with our two major international competitors, Japan and Germany, we find cause for concern,"
says Lowell W. Steele, manager of research and development
planning for General Electric Company. General Electric
estimated capital needs of industry at $351 billion a year from
1977 through 1980. That compared with $182 billion spent in
1974.

All the various capital needs were added up in a 1974–75
study by the New York Stock Exchange as shown in figure
5–4, for the period 1974–85, the Exchange estimated private capital needs at $4.5 trillion and public requirements at
$175 billion. The grand total was $4.7 trillion. In constant
dollars, that would be double the amount spent in the
previous twelve years. A Commerce Department study re-
leased in December, 1975, came up with $1.4 trillion as the
amount needed for private fixed investment between 1971
and 1980. This amounted to 11.4 percent of GNP. "This
percentage is considerably higher than the 10.4 percent
characteristic of the 1965–70 period," the Commerce Study
noted. To make up for lost time, the paper added, spending
after 1975 would have to total $986 billion or twelve percent
of GNP.

All the studies indicate more capital will be needed than will
be available if past trends continue. From 1977 through 1980,
General Electric said, internal funds and borrowing would
fall short of needs by $60 billion. The Commerce paper

FIGURE 5-4. Sources and Uses of Funds—1974-85 (in billions of dollars)

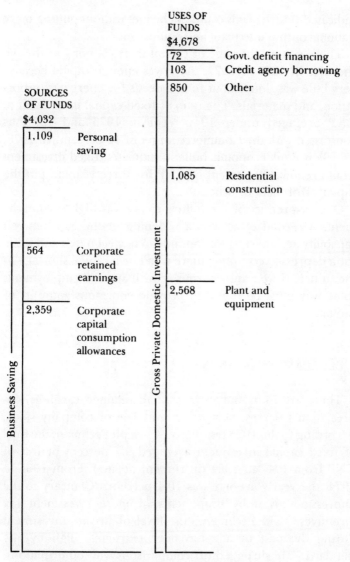

Source: New York Stock Exchange, "The Capital Needs and Savings Potential of the U.S. Economy," September 1974.

indicated future needs could not be met without putting more national output into plant and equipment.

There was no shortage of capital in 1975, nor was there a shortage in 1976 or 1977; there was enough capital because very little was done about future needs for energy, transportation, and materials. The ratio of fixed capital investment to GNP averaged under 10 percent in 1976 and 1977, as contrasted with the Commerce target of 12 percent. In 1978, a Mellon Bank economic bulletin estimated fixed investment would require 30 percent of GNP for three years to put the capital effort back on schedule.

One by-product of the failure to act was high unemployment. A second effect was a widening of the gap between capability and need. If we continue to neglect needs and settle for a depressed economy, there won't be a capital shortage in the future. If we want vigorous growth and full employment, some way must be found to provide enormous amounts of capital.

DECREASED EARNINGS

There are four sources of capital: retained earnings, depreciation reserves, borrowing, and sale of company stock. According to the 1975 testimony of Joseph Pechman, the total of fixed capital investment averaged 9.7 percent or less of GNP from 1947 to 1964 (in current dollars). From 1965 to 1974, the yearly average was 10.4 percent. "Contrary to the impression given by proponents of more investment tax incentives," said Pechman, "the level of private investment during the past decade has been extremely high by any standard." He shrugged off comparisons with other nations, saying they were in earlier stages of development.

Pechman saw as significant the fact that the capital share

has not declined, and he is not alone in remarking on this point. "The percentage of capital formation to GNP hasn't changed in the past thirty years," said F. W. Hickman, Assistant Secretary of the Treasury for tax policy. However, Hickman went on to make another point: "What there really is, is a shortage of retained earnings."

While the capital share of GNP has remained constant, there is evidence this share has been inadequate. As Hickman indicated, however, part of the problem has been the composition of capital input. In 1960, table 5–1 shows, more than 70 percent of corporate funds came from internal sources. By 1974, the internal share was down to 41 percent. There was a sharp reversal of this trend in 1975 as business pulled in its

TABLE 5-1. Sources of Funds—Nonfarm, Nonfinancial, Corporate, and Business (in billions of dollars)

YEAR	TOTAL	INTERNAL	EXTERNAL	EXTERNAL PERCENTAGE OF TOTAL
1960	$ 47.6	$ 34.7	$ 12.9	27.1
1961	54.3	35.3	19.1	34.8
1962	58.8	41.6	17.2	29.2
1963	66.0	44.5	21.4	32.4
1964	72.3	50.1	22.2	30.7
1965	90.9	56.1	34.9	38.4
1966	96.9	60.5	36.4	37.6
1967	93.7	61.3	32.4	34.6
1968	114.5	62.3	52.1	45.5
1969	118.4	61.7	56.7	47.1
1970	104.3	58.9	45.5	43.6
1971	127.1	68.6	58.5	46.0
1972	152.9	80.8	72.2	47.2
1973	180.7	83.8	96.9	53.6
1974	180.7	75.7	105.0	58.1
1975	148.4	107.8	40.6	27.4
1976	213.5	125.8	87.7	41.0

Source: Federal Reserve Board.

horns. By 1977, despite a subpar capital recovery, business was going back into hock.

The shortage of internal cash has been partly due to the decline in the share of profits in the national income. Employee compensation has been gaining at the expense of profits, and no reversal of this trend is in sight. With productivity lagging and inflation raging, unions continue to demand big pay increases. The wage push can have devastating effects on individual industries. There is often no connection between particular wages and particular prices and profits. The steel industry was cutting prices in 1977, but steel employment costs went up by 11 percent. As a result, steel companies made no money in 1977.

By and large, however, business seems resigned to the fact that wages are going to keep going up as long as prices keep going up. And prices are going to keep rising as long as there are big federal deficits. The deficits are financed by printing more dollars—hence inflation. According to many business spokesmen, the remedy for inflation is a cut in government spending. And the answer to the profit and capital shortages is a cut in business taxes; these two are clearly related. "The most important recommendation is a permanent reduction in corporate income tax rates—three percentage points this year and another percentage point in 1980," Reginald Jones told Congress on March 8, 1978. (The 1978 Revenue Act has since cut the top corporate tax rate to 46 percent, a reduction of two percentage points.)

Periodically there will be charges that business is dodging all, or most, of its taxes. According to Representative Charles A. Vanik (D., Ohio), the effective income tax rate of corporations in 1971 was 23 percent. Vanik said five corporations, including Alcoa, paid no federal income tax that year. The effective federal rate for U. S. Steel was 7.6 percent, he said.

Government Policy and Capital Formation

Vanik's overall figure doesn't jibe with that of the Commerce Department. The official statistics show that federal and state income taxes took 41 percent of corporate earnings in 1971. In most recent years, the effective rate has been a little over or under that level. In 1977, U. S. corporations earned $171 billion before taxes. Federal and state income taxes came to $69 million, or 40 percent. Dividends took $41 billion, which left $61 billion in retained earnings.

Corporate taxes are high. The United States gets a larger percentage of its revenue from corporations than do Sweden, Great Britain, and many other countries. Only Japan and Australia get more of their tax money from business income than the United States (see table 5–2).

On the surface, however, it doesn't appear there has been any real shortage of after-tax profits. Through three quarters

TABLE 5-2.   Source of Tax Revenue—1972

| | TAXES AS % OF GNP | SHARE OF TOTAL TAXES | |
		INDIVIDUAL INCOME %	CORPORATE INCOME %
Norway	45.7	27	2
Denmark	44.8	48	2
Sweden	43.9	42	4
Netherlands	41.8	28	7
Austria	37.0	23	4
Germany	36.0	28	5
France	35.8	11	6
Belgium	35.2	27	7
United Kingdom	34.7	32	7
Canada	33.5	34	11
Italy	31.1	13	7
United States	28.1	34	11
Australia	24.3	38	16
Switzerland	24.1	33	8
Japan	21.1	26	24

Source: Organization for Economic Cooperation and Development.

in 1977, after-tax profits of manufacturers were over 13 percent of equity and over 5 percent of sales. The profit ratios were in line with those of past periods. The problem, says business, is that the all the numbers are wrong. Profits are overstated, and costs are understated. The result, it's argued, is gross overtaxation.

UNDERSTATED DEPRECIATION, OVERSTATED PROFITS

This view of overstated profits and understated costs is now being substantiated by the government. According to the Commerce Department, as shown in figure 5–5, the "phantom" profits based on inflation of inventory values added $14.8 billion to corporate profits in 1977. Another $14.9 billion was added by the understatement of depreciation, also due to inflation. The 1978 pattern was similar. Profits after taxes rose by about $16 billion. The inventory profit increased by nearly $10 billion. The understatement of depreciation increased by $3 billion. When these items were deducted, the tax rate on corporated income was over 49 percent in 1977. Retained earnings were reduced from $58 billion to $29 billion. "The real return on investment for nonfinancial corporations after removing the effects of phantom inventory profits and underdepreciation has fallen from 9.9 percent after taxes in 1965 to about 4 percent in 1977," said GE chairman Reginald Jones.

Inventory profits, as the name suggests, come from the fact that material bought at one price is valued at a higher price when the products in which it's incorporated are eventually sold. With rapid inflation, this kind of accounting can generate huge sums. In 1974, when inflation was particularly bad, the profit on inventory was nearly $40 billion. When profits

FIGURE 5-5. Effect of Inflation on Corporate Profits (in billions of dollars)

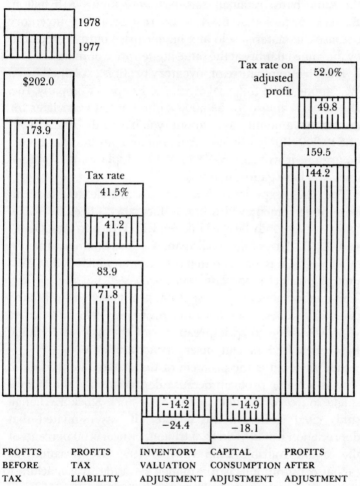

1978
1977

$202.0
173.9

Tax rate on adjusted profit
52.0%
49.8

159.5
144.2

Tax rate
41.5%
41.2

83.9
71.8

−14.2
−24.4

−14.9
−18.1

| PROFITS BEFORE TAX | PROFITS TAX LIABILITY | INVENTORY VALUATION ADJUSTMENT | CAPITAL CONSUMPTION ADJUSTMENT | PROFITS AFTER ADJUSTMENT |

Source: Department of Commerce.

were adjusted for this amount (and for underdepreciation), the tax rate for nonfinancial corporations was 69 percent. On the same basis, retained earnings were minus $16 billion. Business argues that there is no real profit on inventory because the material sold at a higher price must be replaced by the same quantity at the same higher price or more.

The phantom nature of inventory profit is explained by A. W. Capone, chief financial officier of Koppers Company, Inc. If you buy a house for $40,000 and sell it ten years later for double that amount, says Capone, you have a theortical profit of $40,000. But if you have to go out and buy another home, he argues, it will cost you $80,000 to duplicate the original unit. You have gained nothing.

The 1974 experience brought a wholesale switch to an accounting remedy which has, in fact, always been available. "Almost everybody bit the bullet on LIFO (Last In First Out)," said E. B. Fitzgerald, chairman, Cutler-Hammer, Inc. In other words, it is assumed that the inventory included in each unit of product is the last item purchased, not the earliest. This method eliminates most of the profit created by inflated inventory values. The inventory profits of 1974 and earlier years were due to widespread use of the more traditional FIFO (First In, First Out) inventory accounting.

Still unsolved is the problem of understated depreciation. This is a major problem because depreciation is the biggest single source of capital. In the New York Stock Exchange study cited earlier in this chapter, it was estimated that depreciation would yield $2.3 trillion, or nearly 60 percent, of the capital available from 1974 to 1985. Depreciation, or capital consumption, is the money set aside as a machine's useful life is expended. The idea is to have enough cash accumulated to replace the machine when its useful life ends. Depreciation charges are considered costs and are not subject to income taxes. If that were not so, the government would be taxing capital. Investors would be better off putting money in the bank. But depreciation is based on original cost. With the rapid inflation of recent years, the amounts set aside have not been anywhere near enough to replace worn-out machines. The deficiency has meant that money classed as retained profit has had to be used for maintaining existing facilities.

A clear example comes from the steel industry. "From 1960 through 1974, the industry invested $24.1 billion," noted Frederick C. Jaicks, chairman of Inland Steel Company. These billions produced no increase in capacity. As a matter of fact, the industry actually contracted over those years. Producing at maximum rates in 1974, the steel industry turned out less metal than its rated capacity in 1960. (The industry has not operated at capacity since 1974.) Of the total spent, $7 billion came from retained steel earnings. Since this money did nothing more than replace old capacity, it can be argued it should have been classed as depreciation, not profit. And since it was not profit, it should not have been taxed.

In theory, a company can depreciate its plant and equipment as fast as it wants. The only hitch is that under the tax law the company must show that its depreciation schedule matches the actual life of the facilities. With actual lives on many machines extending forty years or more, inflation would create an enormous depreciation gap if payments had to be spread over the period of use.

The government recognizes there is a legitimate need to recover capital before a machine is expended. Accordingly, guidelines have been established for useful lives. If the guidelines are followed, a company need not justify its depreciation. In addition, there are various plans for accelerating depreciation. In 1962 the Kennedy administration shortened depreciation lives and established the 7 percent investment credit. According to the Commerce Department, these changes corrected an understatement dating back to

1929. From 1962 through 1973, said Commerce, depreciation was overstated by $1 billion in most years and by more than $3.5 billion in five years.

In 1974 alone, however, consumer prices rose 12 percent, and wholesale prices went up 20 percent. What this meant to replacement costs is shown by an estimate of Bethlehem Steel Corporation. To have duplicated a plate mill, installed in 1962, would have cost six times the original price fourteen years later. Again, according to the Commerce Department, the cumulative effect of inflation resulted in an understatement of depreciation by $2.1 billion in 1974, $12.2 billion in 1975, $14.4 billion in 1976, $14.9 billion in 1977, and $18.1 billion in 1978. That is over $60 billion in only five years.

In calling for more liberal depreciation rules, business argues that other nations have more realistic schedules. "Whereas the U. S. cost recovery figure for the first three years stands at 55 percent," said Jones (it is now 60 percent), "Canada is 100 percent, France 90 percent, Italy 65 percent, Japan 64 percent, Sweden 96 percent, and the United Kingdom 100 percent."

There was a modest revision of depreciation terms in 1970. More significant have been changes in the investment tax credit. Under the Revenue Adjustment Act of 1975, the maximum credit for qualified facilities was boosted from 4 percent to 10 percent for utilities and from 7 percent to 10 percent for all other businesses. Under the Tax Reform Act of 1976, the 10 percent investment credit was extended to 1980, and in the 1978 Revenue Act it was made "permanent."

From the business standpoint, one trouble with the investment credit is that it has been a favorite tool for regulating the economy. The credit was installed in 1962, temporarily suspended in 1966, removed in 1969, and reinstated in 1971. Business people say this kind of juggling has made planning impossible. It remains to be seen whether the latest change reflects a new attitude on government's part.

The business case for faster depreciation is weakened by the reluctance of companies to show the overstatement of earnings. Accelerated depreciation is used for tax purposes, but depreciation is computed on a straight-line basis in reports to stockholders. In other words, companies say the tax rules force an overstatement of earnings, and then the same companies make a further overstatement in their annual reports.

There is some logic to this practice. If a company launched a large capital program, the concentrated effect of accelerated depreciation would distort earnings. The greatest subtraction of earnings would occur in the start-up period, when new facilities were yielding the least return. But the real reason for dual accounting is the split personality of management. Companies want to look as poor as possible to tax collectors and unions and as rich as possible to investors. The desire to appear prosperous explains why many companies stayed with FIFO accounting even though it added to their taxes.

In the depreciation area, the difficulty of looking rich and poor at the same time is solved by keeping two sets of books, a practice deplored by Fitzgerald of Cutler-Hammer. "We are giving our enemies an inflated view of our earnings," he said in 1975. Cutler-Hammer uses the same accounting for tax and reporting purposes. F. W. Hickman of the Treasury warned that dual accounting made for a cynical congressional reaction to proposals for tax reform. "Why should we believe them when they're lying to their stockholders?" the legislators ask. It's possible a lot of companies are kidding themselves as well. Taxes are a cost of doing business. If companies are being overtaxed, the businesslike thing would be to set prices in a manner that reflects this extra cost and provides an adequate profit.

One reason that doesn't happen is that there is fairly widespread ignorance of manufacturing economics. "They don't know their costs," one company will complain about another in a time of price weakness. According to one authority, half the machinery builders in the country are still using straight-line depreciation, even for tax purposes.

In 1977, the Securities and Exchange Commission began forcing companies to look at their true full costs. The regular earnings report must now be supplemented by an estimate of the effect of inflation on depreciation and earnings.

Even with conventional accounting, companies could do a better job of presenting their earnings. In the first quarter of 1979, the profit of National Steel Corporation was up more than 700 percent from the first quarter of 1978. Year-to-year percentage gains of this kind invariably make headlines. Companies complain that the gains often reflect unusually low starting points. In National's case, there was practically no profit in the first quarter of 1978.

A more accurate picture of profitability could be obtained if earnings were related to sales or investment. In National's case, earnings in the first quarter of 1979 came to less than 2 percent of sales. This relationship is rarely included in the reports of companies to the public. You have to do some digging, for example, to find that the 'windfall' profits of the oil industry in 1978 came to a little over 4 percent of sales.

From a tax standpoint, what's needed are rules that minimize the effect of inflation on depreciation. These should be supplemented by a further lowering of corporate tax rates. At the same time, companies must begin basing their prices on true costs to a greater extent. The ideal solution, of course, would be to end inflation. This hasn't proved an easy task, but neither will it be easy to develop a tax and price structure that maintains an adequate capital supply during inflationary periods. Chapter 8 will discuss proposals for using tax incentives to moderate the wage-push aspect of inflation. Tax reductions for business should be considered in the same light. A tax cut relieves price pressures by reducing the cost of government to business.

THE COMPETITION FOR MONEY

Corresponding with the decrease in internal cash generation has been a growing reliance on external sources for capital. Figure 5–6 shows that, from $302 billion in 1960, corporate debt went to $1.4 trillion in 1976. The ratio of debt to equity for manufacturers went from 20 percent in 1965 to 47 percent in 1974. The money borrowed by business comes from the same pool used by government to cover deficits. It is this fact that puts capital formation on a collision course with the egalitarian movement. To leave enough capital for private investment, government must hold down its social spending.

FIGURE 5-6. Corporate Debt (in billions of dollars)

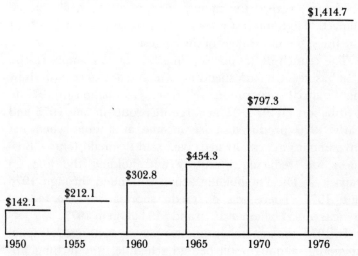

Source: Department of Commerce.

The money used by government and business comes from savings. The New York Stock Exchange estimated these would amount to $1.1 trillion from 1974 to 1985. In computing the need for borrowed money, the Exchange made the wildly optimistic assumption that federal deficits would average $3.5 billion a year through 1985 and total $42 billion over the twelve-year period. (Exchange officials said they were deliberately conservative.)

The 1974 deficit was $10.7 billion. That brought the total deficit from 1970 through 1974 to more than $68 billion. This seemed a lot until 1975, when the deficit for one year was more than $70 billion. At this stage, there were stern warnings of a credit crunch. Treasury Secretary William Simon predicted "vicious competition" for money when the economy returned to normal. "Small and intermediate companies won't even be able to finance inventory," said Martin Stone, president of Monogram Industries. James J. Needham, who was then president of the New York Stock Exchange, agreed the money squeeze would have uneven impact: "High interest rates mean survival not necessarily of the fittest but more likely of the biggest."

The crunch didn't develop in 1975 for the simple reason that business cut back spending. The use of external funds by nonfinancial corporations fell from $105 billion in 1974 to $40 billion in 1975. "The surge in profits in late 1975 and early 1976 produced more income at a time when net investment was actually negative," said Reginald Jones. "Business was reducing inventory and holding the line on capacity." The line-holding action continued through 1976 and 1977. There was no credit shortage despite federal deficits of $54 billion in 1976 and $49 billion in 1977.

In 1978, the general economic recovery continued. Capital spending, although still behind schedule, was inching upward. In this setting, the federal deficit was coming down, but was still extremely high. In the first quarter of 1978, the deficit was $55 billion on an annual basis.

This ran counter to the theory that federal deficits create no credit problems, because they occur only in slack periods when business borrowing is down. When the economy revives and business wants credit, according to this same theory, increased tax revenues wipe out the federal deficits. "The theory goes that we run deficits during periods of business contraction, to stimulate the economy and offset these deficits with surpluses during periods of expansion," said William Simon in 1975. "But the hard fact is that we have had only one year of budget surplus in the last sixteen years."

The 1978 combination of economic expansion and a large deficit brought cries of alarm from the banking community. At about the same time, inflation showed signs of heating up. Also at this time, in the middle of 1978, interest rates moved up. The prime bank lending rate went from 6.1 percent to 9 percent. This gave the appearance of the overcrowding in the credit market that Secretary Simon warned of.

It's questionable, however, that the early interest rise was a response to excessive demand. Consumer prices rose sharply in early 1978. The federal discount rate was increased two points. The fact is, much of the rise was due to a deliberate Federal Reserve Board policy of pushing up rates to slow monetary growth.

If the initial interest spurt was contrived, the eventual problem will be real enough. A genuine boom with uncontrolled government spending will bring vicious competition for money. To ward off this conflict, business proposes tax policies that encourage national frugality. "Essentially, the task of accumulating enough capital means that people must save more and consume less," said Needham.

The big savers are corporations and affluent people. Those who save least are poor people. In short, government must check the rising transfer of income from the rich to the poor.

Stated that way, the business slogan doesn't sound like a very good one for a rising politician. In 1978, nevertheless, people were getting elected on pledges that came very close to the business proposition.

EQUITY FINANCING

In its capital projection, the New York Stock Exchange said equity financing through the sale of new common stock, should provide $250 billion of the $800 billion needed in outside money over twelve years and that net equity purchases will fall short of the goal by about $7 billion a year. General Electric concluded that half the outside money required through 1980 would have to come from equity financing, leaving roughly $60 billion a year to come from new share issues. As Reginald Jones of GE said, "It would take some bull market to provide $60 billion a year in new issues." It would, indeed, take a reversal of past trends for common stock to provide a significant amount of new capital. In the twenty years prior to 1975, equity financing provided an average of $3 billion a year. That was less than 4 percent of the total input.

Companies have avoided equity financing partly because the tax structure favors borrowing. "Interest and dividends are both sources of capital," Jones said, "but interest is tax deductible and dividends are not. Hence, the tax structure is pushing corporations into debt."

In the early Seventies, low stock prices also discouraged equity financing. The total market value of U. S. Steel's common stock was $2.5 billion. (There had been no change by early 1979). That was less than the amount needed to build a plant that would increase U. S. Steel's capacity 10 percent. "Steelmaking capacity can be bought on the stock market for one-tenth its replacement cost," said Heath Larry, who was then vice chairman of U. S. Steel.

As to why investors should have so little interest in owning corporations, Jones said, "With profit margins and return on investment declining, savers prefer to lend their money instead of risking it in equities." This preference has received a big push from the banks and the Federal Reserve. Every time the price of hamburger goes up 1 percent, the bankers start agitating for higher interest rates—and as the rates go up, the incentive to invest in common stock goes down.

Since 1970, it hasn't seemed to matter what happened to profits; stock prices have tended downward. "The stock market has declined and over five million investors have dropped out of the market," said Congressman William A. Steiger (R., Wisc.) in 1978. These investors must be drawn back, said the New York Stock Exchange. "The household sector—particularly the individual investor—holds the key to overcoming the capital supply insufficiency."

Equity financing was relatively unimportant even in the old bull markets. Why, then, should it matter that the stock market has dried up as a source of funds? Partly because equity has always been important in the formation of new companies. And new companies tend to be innovative ones, formed because some guy has an idea and is willing to bet his savings that this will make him a millionaire.

CAPITAL GAINS TAX CUTS: WHO BENEFITS?

In Congressman Steiger's opinion, the incentive to create has been choked off by taxation. "High technology industries and venture investors are convinced that the root cause of inadequate capital is the Tax Reform Act of 1969, the law which increased the tax on capital gains. In 1968, 300 high technology companies were started. In 1976, there were none. In 1969, 698 firms with a net worth under $5 million raised $1.4 billion in capital. In 1975, four firms raised $15 million. And in 1977, thirty firms raised $118 million." There is no question that increased capital gains taxes have made it more difficult to get rich quick. There is no question, either, that the desire for wealth has generated great amounts of progress; and with little hope for fulfilling that desire, economic advancement is thwarted.

Steiger's corrective was a cut in capital gains taxes. Also proposed, by others, is elimination of "double taxation" of dividends. The same income, says Jones, is taxed "once when the corporate income is taxed to the corporation and again when the dividends from that income are taxed to the shareholders."

A 1978 Congressional proposal called for partial integration of corporate and individual taxes on dividends in 1979. Among those unenthusiastic about this approach was Congressman Steiger. "We should bear in mind that high-growth companies, the ones that provide new jobs, pay almost no dividends." As has been said, Steiger's proposed cut in capital gains taxes was blasted by the administration as a boon to millionaires. Supporters of the proposal responded with examples of benefits for middle-income homeowners. The New York Stock Exchange periodically releases figures showing that stocks are owned by lots of low-income people—10 million with incomes under $15,000 in 1975.

Nevertheless, it is probably true that direct stock ownership is concentrated in high-income hands. According to a 1974 Wharton School of Finance study for the Commerce Department, "the 1 percent of U. S. families with the largest personal income accounted for 47 percent of the dividend income received by individuals and 51 percent of the market value owned by all families. The 10 percent of families with the largest incomes accounted for 71 percent of the dividend income and 74 percent of market value."

Stock ownership has probably been dispersed by the recent exodus of individuals from the market and the growing dominance of institutions. Pension funds would certainly tend to give indirect ownership of stock to a great many low-income people. But it is doubtless true that wealthy people own a large share of the wealth represented by corporate stocks. This pattern has much to do with labor's attitude toward tax concessions for corporations. "Tax benefits tilted toward those who receive dividend income and sell corporate stock automatically benefit a small group of the super-wealthy," said George Meany, who might have added that organized labor has shown no great interest in broadening the ownership base. Profit-sharing and stock-distribution plans have never appealed to unions. These are fine in prosperous times, but workers aren't keen on sharing the skimpy earnings or losses of lean years.

The unions show good sense in demanding cash on the barrel head and letting others get rich—or poor—on the stock market. The fact is, business is a risky business. British economist John Maynard Keynes touched on market uncertainties with these words: "It is generally agreed that casinos in the public interest should be inaccessible and expensive. And perhaps the same is true for the stock market."

The tax consequences of the effect of inflation on equity values were outlines by Harvard's Martin Feldstein in the *Wall Street Journal* (July 27, 1978): "We found that in 1973 individuals paid capital gains tax on $4.6 billion of nominal capital gains on corporate stock. When the cost of these shares are adjusted for the increase in the consumer price level since they were purchased, this gain becomes a loss of nearly $1 billion. The $4.6 billion of nominal capital gains resulted in a tax liability of $1.1 billion. The tax liability on the real capital gains would have been only $661 million. Inflation thus raised tax liabilities by nearly $500 million, approximately doubling the overall effective tax rate on corporate stock capital gains."

With regard to taxes on business, a Census Bureau study assumed that half the state and local levies were passed on to consumers and that over the long run, the same thing happened to one-third of the corporate income tax. The Brookings Institution study by George Break and Joseph Pechman *(Federal Tax Reform: The Impossible Dream?)* agreed there was a pass-through, but said the amount could not be pinpointed. "There is no accurate way of measuring the extent to which property and corporate profit taxes, though nominally levied on property values and income, are actually shifted to consumers."

It follows from this that a portion of any tax relief for business will be passed on to consumers. It does not necessarily follow that benefits retained by business will be passed back to owners. Tax savings applied to pollution abatement, for example, will produce no monetary gain for the owners.

Actually, the ties between many large corporations and their stockholders have become very tenuous. Most of the trading in stocks has nothing to do with raising fresh capital. In 1972, four billion shares with a value of $160 billion were traded on the New York Stock Exchange. That compared with the average of $3 billion a year raised by equity financing over the past two years. The trading seems to be more of a separate game than anything based on corporate operations and corporate values. "We don't have anything to do with the stock market," said R. A. DePalma, treasurer in 1973 of

Rockwell International. "Our shares are sitting out there and people are trading. That's just shooting craps."

The remoteness of stockholders from corporations showed up in the late Sixties when conglomerate take-overs were facilitated by the small amount of stock owned by company officers and directors. In Europe, the fact that nobody really owns a corporation is pointed up by union representation on boards. In this country, members of the clergy and college professors are appearing as directors. Shareholder meetings of Gulf, Rockwell, and other large corporations are taken up by ethical discussions on the company's position on South Africa, abortion, nuclear power, and the like.

Company executives, however, are potential beneficiaries of corporate tax cuts. Compensation experts Towers, Perrin, Forster & Crosby, checked 100 large companies. Of these, 86 offered executives some kind of short-term incentive payment. All the big companies offered stock options or long-term incentives. To the extent that options are in lieu of other compensation, they have been no real bargain. The stock market has been too whimsical to provide any assurance that good financial performance will be rewarded.

It would be desirable and the natural thing for more people to own stocks. Corporations are assets of the whole country. If General Motors failed, it would be a disaster for the whole country. If the financial dependence of everyone on business could be formalized, it would ease tensions on tax, social, and wage questions.

Whatever the means, some way must be found to provide more capital. The existing industrial base is badly in need of renovation. There are vast needs ahead. Part of the answer to the problems now facing business lies in a tax structure that preserves more of the seed corn.

THE 1978 TAX BILL

On October 16, 1978, Congress passed a tax package billed as an $18.7 billion reduction. Of this amount, $12.7 billion was in the form of individual cuts, $3.7 billion went to business, and $2.2 billion was in the form of lower capital gains taxes. The bill fell short of conservative hopes. "The taxpapers have been had again," wrote the *Wall Street Journal* the following day. With Social Security taxes due to go up $8.5 billion in 1979 and with inflation expected to add $13.5 billion, said the *Journal*, there would be a net increase of $3.3 billion. Senator Howard Baker (R., Tenn.) said every family making over $8,000 would be paying higher taxes in 1979.

The complaints of conservatives in 1978 were matched by the denunciations of such liberal organizations as Ralph Nader's Tax Reform Group. "The tax bill reverses over ten years of tax reform efforts," said Ralph Brandon, director of the Nader group. "The long effort to eliminate the special treatment of capital gains—the biggest loophole in the tax system for the wealthy—would be dealt a knockout blow unless the President rejects the bill" *(Wall Street Journal,* Oct. 16, 1978).

It will probably be years before anyone really knows what the 1978 tax law means. The estimates of dollar reductions are all based on a frozen economy. As Jack Kemp has repeatedly pointed out, the effect on tax revenue will depend on the effect of cuts on the economy.

One thing the 1978 action did do: it refuted the charge of liberals that it is easy to cut taxes. Legislators would still be wrangling had they not faced an adjournment deadline. As it was, a large and complex law was passed in the bleary hours of the morning. Decisions that could have sweeping effects were made in a few hours' time.

Among other things, Congress extended the negative income tax—something few people know exists. Under the old law, a low-income taxpayer with a dependent was entitled to a credit equal to 10 percent of the first $4,000 earned. The 1978 act made the credit permanent and lifted the amount to 10 percent of the first $5,000 earned. If the credit exceeds a person's tax liability, the difference is paid out by the government.

All in all, the 1978 tax bill would have to be considered favorable to the conservative position and particularly so for business. The top corporate income tax rate was cut from 48 to 46 percent. That was one point shy of what business sought and what the Carter administration proposed. The administration had also called for another one-point reduction in 1980.

Another major victory for business was the liberalizing of the investment credit. This had been scheduled to drop to 7 percent in 1981. The existing 10 percent was made permanent. In ten-point stages, the amount of the tax liability that can be offset by the credit was raised to 90 percent. The credit, formerly restricted to machinery, is now available to repair or renovate buildings that have been in use more than twenty years. Under the new law, the full credit is available for pollution-abatement devices amortized over five years. The old rule reduced the credit to 5 percent when a fast write-off was taken.

These provisions were all pretty much in line with the Carter administration's original tax proposal. Not proposed by the administration and strenuously opposed at first was the reduction in the maximum capital gains tax rate from 49 to 28 percent. The lower "normal" capital gains rates are also cut. The amount excluded from regular tax rates is lifted from 50 to 60 percent.

The new law allows a tax-free profit of $100,000 on a home sale once in a person's lifetime after age 55. This profit is excluded from the minimum income tax. Special provisions governing home sales by the elderly are also available to those over 55. The old minimum was 65.

The new capital gains provisions are favorable to businessmen as individuals. They will be less important to most businesses, but they are calculated to encourage investors in the formation of capital. Congressman Steiger, who almost single-handedly brought about the capital gains reform, feels it will make a big difference in the formation of new companies.

Apart from the new provisions on environmental facilities, nothing was done to liberalize business depreciation. A proposal for more rapid depreciation of small business assets were dropped out in the last-minute squeeze. However, all the pro-business proposals of the administration were approved. In addition, there was the reduction in capital gains taxes. A year earlier, it's doubtful many people would have predicted so favorable an outcome for business.

For individuals, the new law raised the personal exemption from $750 to $1,000. The standard deduction was increased $100 for single taxpayers and $200 for married taxpayers. There were rate cuts in some middle-income brackets. To cushion the effects of inflation, the tax brackets were widened. The 25 brackets under the old structure were reduced to sixteen for single people and to fifteen for couples.

Most significant, possibly, was what Congress almost did. The Kemp-Roth bill, which was originally regarded as a fly-by-night thing, was very nearly passed. The bill itself was defeated in the Senate by a 60-to-36 vote. "But with barely a blush," wrote *Time Magazine,* October 23, 1978, "the Democrats last week rammed through an amendment introduced by Georgia conservative Sam Nunn that could cut taxes

$164.5 billion by 1983. . . . Republican Senator William Roth of Delaware promptly signed as a co-sponsor and laughingly passed out cigars in honor of the first 'Son of Kemp-Roth.'"

The reductions were made contingent on limitations to federal spending and deficits.

Business complains that other industrial nations are outstripping the United States in productivity growth partly because of this country's prejudicial tax policies and shortsighted social spending programs. Obsolescence brought on by lack of investment money is affecting many of the major business areas already, and the picture for the future looks even worse. Of the four traditional sources of capital two—retained earnings and depreciation reserves—are directly lessened by taxes, and the other two—borrowing and sale of company stock—are indirectly weakened because of the risks connected with inflation, itself seen by business as a stepchild of government economic policies.

But the future for economic growth might not be all black. The 1978 tax bill can be seen as favorable to business, with its cut in the top corporate income tax rate, liberalizing of the investment credit, and reduction in the maximum capital gains tax. Tax changes directly benefiting individuals can have an indirect benefit for business, if more people are thereby encourage to become investors.

Perhaps the government is beginning to believe what business has known all along—that the best social insurance is a strong economy.

Chapter 6

GOVERNMENT REGULATION

I ncome transfer and government regulation have much in common: both hold down the production of goods and services, both tend to increase the size and power of government, and, in the opinion of many, both pose threats to liberty.

Regulation does one more thing: while holding down production, it increases the need for goods and services. At a time when there is a special need to boost output, regulators have decreed that more and more of our resources must go to protecting the environment, insuring health, complying with product standards, and sheltering endangered species. In terms of both subtracting wealth and increasing needs, regulation has moved from the nuisance to the oppressive stage.

Needless to say, regulators argue otherwise. Regardless of any side effects, they say, government guidance is necessary to preserve and enhance the quality of life. It is difficult to argue against this proposition on a piecemeal basis. The regulators have many laudable aims. However, the aggregate effect is the imposition of a philosophy that government knows best. This is something to be resisted—not only because it usurps the right of the individual to make a free choice in a free market, but also because, overall, government *doesn't* know best. Life is shabby and shoddy in countries where quality is established by government edict. This is because bureaucrats lack common sense. This is not a matter of individual intelligence. Isolated from profit and loss pressures, the bureaucrats are unable to perceive broad effects. They are unable to recognize priorities or probabilities.

FREE CHOICE AND REGULATION

The issue of free choice comes up in the matter of safety equipment for autos. According to the National Highway Traffic Safety Administration, only 19.7 percent of new car owners used their safety belts in 1977. That meant 80 percent of the owners were paying for a device they didn't want, even though the amount paid was not insignificant. On 1976 General Motors models, safety features added $385 to the average price and emission controls another $215. By 1978, the total addition was $666. And the sum will rise: the regulators are itching to put air bags on cars; emission standards are being tightened. GM estimates it is spending $1 billion a year to comply with government regulators. Ford Motor Company says the whole auto industry may have to spend $40 billion in the next four or five years to meet the product standards established by government.

These dollars come out of the consumer's pocket. Given a choice it's doubtful that the average consumer would shell out $666 for safety and pollution equipment. There were few takers when GM offered an air bag option on certain models, and there was a similar response when they tried to sell a kit that enabled motorists to put emission controls on old models. The clearest expression of preference came when the government specified interlocking systems that forced people to use seat belts. A storm of protest brought hasty action by Congress to detach the systems.

Advocates of mandatory safety justify their position by saying an injured driver becomes a burden on society; society, therefore, has the right to demand precautionary measures. That may be true, but the same rationale could be used to support rules for everything from playing tennis to eating ice cream. The inference is that the Constitutional guarantee of freedom is limited to wise, moderate actions.

It can be argued that emission controls for cars fall into a different class. Here, the individual is not simply exposing *himself* to injury—he is polluting the air inhaled by others. However, many of the recipients of the pollution are the same people who do the polluting. A collective decision to breathe smog rather than pay for emission controls may be wrong, but it should at least be noted. As it is, the most stringent emission standards are being imposed without the least concern for public preference.

But why should anyone object to spending money for such desirable things as clean air and safety? Very simply, because people want to spend the money for other items. In the absence of regulation, some of the items purchased would doubtless be frivolous. For the nation as a whole, the regulatory explosion is subtracting resources that are urgently needed elsewhere. Government is imposing special demands on an economy that is short of energy, pinched for capital, and plagued by inflation. This is one of the rubs of the regulatory crunch. Vast sums are spent with no weighing of the benefits to be obtained and no consideration of benefits from alternate uses of funds.

Likewise, there is little consideration of probabilities. It is possible that nuclear power plants will harm someone in the future. There are arguments on both sides of this question. However, the fact is that exactly two persons have been killed so far by nuclear plants in the United States (the deaths occurred in an Army installation). The possibility of a nuclear catastrophe has to be considered remote. On the other hand, it is almost certain that there will be power shortages if nuclear construction is not accelerated.

THE COSTS OF REGULATION

To adequately judge the benefits and costs, regulatory aims must be considered in the light of all the options, the costs, the consequences, and the probabilities. There is rarely an argument when each regulation is considered by itself. For example, viewed as an isolated objective, there is no limit to the degree of air cleanliness that should be required. After all, we all have to breathe it, and so do our children. Government agencies favor this view, but it is one that appears to ignore the fact that the $1 billion General Motors spends on regulation could be used to pay 22,000 workers.

This kind of trade-off is taking place throughout the economy. In 1978 the Occupational Safety and Health Administration proposed coke oven regulations that could add as much as $13 a ton to the price of steel. For a nation that chews up more than 100 million tons of steel a year, that one bit of regulation would be extremely costly.

The Commerce Department estimated that business would spend $7.2 billion on pollution abatement in 1978. Writing in *Regulation* magazine (May/June 1978), Murray L. Weidenbaum of Washington University placed the 1976 cost of energy and environmental regulation at more than $8.3 billion. He estimated the 1978 administrative cost of 41 federal agencies at $4.5 billion. The total cost of federal regulation, including administration and compliance, came to $65.5 billion in 1976 (see table 6–1). In considering the most conservative cost numbers, remember it would take only $9 billion to raise all working-age families above the poverty line.

Consider, too, the capital drain. The steel industry, which made no money in 1977 and is desperately in need of modernization, spent $534 million on pollution abatement in 1977, $489 million in 1976, and $453 million in 1975. Through 1976, the steel industry had $4.9 billion invested in environmental equipment. By 1985, the total is expected to be $9.8 billion with no provision for expansion.

The time consumed by the regulatory process is extremely costly. The classic case was the coal-fired Kaiporowits power project in Utah. When it was proposed

TABLE 6-1. Estimated Cost of Federal Regulation in 1976 (calendar year, in millions of dollars)

	ADMINISTRATION COST	COMPLIANCE COST	TOTAL
Consumer safety and health	$1,516	$ 5,094	$ 6,610
Job safety and working conditions	483	4,015	4,498
Energy and the environment	612	7,760	8,372
Financial regulation	104	1,118	1,222
Industry specific	474	26,322	26,796
Paperwork	(^{1})	18,000	18,000
Total	$3,189	$62,309	$65,498

[1] Included in other sources.

Source: Murray Weidenbaum, "On Estimating Regulatory Costs," *Regulation,* May/June 1978, p. 17. From Weidenbaum and DeFina, *The Cost of Federal Regulation of Economic Activity,* Washington, D.C., American Enterprise Institute, May 1978. Copyright © 1978 American Enterprise Institute.

in 1965, the project was to have cost $500 million for 5,000 megawatts; after spending ten years and $20 million in a futile attempt to clear the project, the utilities decided it was no longer economically feasible, as by then the cost had risen to $750 million for 3,000 megawatts. By late 1978 U. S. Steel had been trying for nearly two years to get environmental clearance for a new mill; during this period, the cost of building the plant was rising at the rate of about $100,000 a day. As of mid-1978, Cities Service had been waiting for two years for approval of a pipeline to transport natural gas from a tight sands formation in Wyoming. The Department of Energy had a backlog of 40,000 such cases, reported *The Wall Street Journal* on August 7, 1978.

Apart from inflating costs, regulatory delays hold back badly needed facilities. Power shortages are likely. Not so widely recognized is the inevitability of a steel shortage, and already in 1978 shortages of aluminum were forcing users to pay premium prices for imported material.

The enervating effects of regulation are difficult to measure but must be significant. The slowing of progress figures to get worse. Covering more than 100 pages in the *Federal Register,* the 1977 amendments to the Clean Air Act bring new complexity and confusion to the environmental field. At the same time, the new provisions are inflexible in the matter of compliance deadlines and noncompliance penalties.

With regard to homes and housing, the regulatory slowdown is very much in evidence. A Rutgers University study completed in July, 1978, showed that the time required to build the average home went from five months in 1970 to thirteen months in 1975. The study said regulation was largely responsible for the stretch-out. It was also noted that every added month increased the cost of the home 1 to 2 percent.

QUARTERLY CONTROL IN A FREE MARKET

In the whole consumer area, regulation has intruded gratuitously on freedom. "Washington rather than Detroit now acts as the representative of the people in the area of personal transportation, and the auto industry has been slow to recognize that fact," said William O. Bourke, executive vice president, Ford Motor Company.

If government were simply conveying the wishes of people, that would be one thing. But, as the seat belt experience showed, government often imposes its own wisdom against the wishes of most people. Obviously, there are areas where the average person isn't competent to detect hazards and flaws in products. As a general proposition, however, it hasn't been shown that regulation produces as high a level of quality as free selection in a free market.

Before the consumerist and environmental movements went into high gear, the free market was bringing a steady improvement in product quality. "The average washing machine now has a life of eleven years," said Stanley Gault of General Electric in 1970. "That compares with seven years in 1950." This position was backed by J. M. Juran, an independent authority on quality control. "For any product line, today's product quality is usually far better than it was years ago," said Juran at the 1970 Technical Conference of the American Society of Quality Control. "Not only are usage factors better; the life is also better. Today's tires, lamps, TV sets—all run longer before failures than their predecessor models."

BUREAUCRATIC BOONDOGGLES

One of the problems in all this is the negative bias of regulation. The tendency is not to act or decide or approve.

This is becoming critical in the pollution field, said John Quarles, former deputy administrator of the Environmental Protection Agency (EPA). In the early days, said Quarles, EPA's emphasis was on cleaning up existing sources. If EPA failed to make a decision, the status quo was simply preserved. Today, continued Quarles, the agency is concentrating on new sources. In this field, indecision will halt construction. "Any inability of the federal system to work will have the ability to hold back private activity," said Quarles.

The natural bureaucratic tendency toward inaction is being enforced by processes that permit public intervention at every step. "The same objections can be raised over and over again," said T. A. Venderslice, senior vice president, power systems, General Electric. "The proponents have to win every round. The opponents need win only once." The opponents have not been backward about asserting their views. When the National Energy Act called for power companies to switch from oil and gas to coal, there was an immediate reaction from those whose only interest was in the soot from coal. "Everybody in the environmental movement rallied round," recalled Richard Grundy, who was on the staff of the Senate Committee on Energy and Natural Resources. "The exemptions for oil and gas use were broadened."

This is just one of many examples of conflicting objectives and a lack of priorities. The government's demand for tight emission controls on cars conflicts with the demand for fuel conservation, and there is a case where one government agency specified that construction vehicles had to be equipped with warning bells; meanwhile, another agency had ruled that workers had to wear ear plugs.

Government officials concede there are flaws in the regulatory process, but they argue that it is unrealistic to talk about doing away with regulation. "If we wish to maintain our commitment to an increasingly complex economic, technological, and social system, it is illusory to think we are going to get away from big government," said Russell E. Train when he was Administrator of EPA. "Major government programs and widespread regulation are inherent in that kind of society . . . . It is a question of how and where we are going to regulate."

In the eyes of business, government is now regulating everywhere to an excessive degree. "There isn't a day in my business life when I'm not harassed by some regulatory agency," said Robert Lauterbach, chairman of Wheeling-Pittsburgh Steel Corporation in 1975. "During the past fifteen years, 236 new federal agencies and departments have been created," said William Renner, president of Alcoa. "Only 21 have been eliminated."

The Council on Wage and Price Stability studied the effect of regulation on the steel industry. "They turned up some 5,600 regulations put out by 27 different agencies," said David M. Roderick, chairman of U. S. Steel. More than anything else, it is the sheer volume of regulation that overwhelms business.

Assuming all the complaints are justified, is there still not an overriding need to protect the health, safety, and environmental quality of the community? "Left unregulated, in a highly advanced industrial society," said Train, "all the normal economic incentives of a competitive, free enterprise system work to encourage the disposal of vast volumes of waste into the environment."

It is true industry once put out vast quantities of waste. John Barker recalls a time when Armco Inc. would dump so much oil in ponds that there would be periodic fires. Head of environmental engineering for Armco, Barker can remember when he got two or three phone calls a week from people who wanted to know why the Miami River was red. It was red because it was receiving tons of iron-bearing material from Armco's plant in Middletown, Ohio. There was also a time when industry employed child labor and operated sweatshops twelve hours a day, seven days a week. That time is past, and so is the day when the Miami River ran red. The river is clean because Armco spent $289 million on pollution control at Middletown. Commitments for most of the cleanup were made *before* the Federal Clean Air Act was passed. One symbolic move was the installation of scrubbers on Middletown open hearths in December of 1970. This was just about the time the federal legislation was enacted, but the pressure for a December start-up came from Armco Chairman Verity, who told his engineers, "I want to say we'll have a white Christmas in 1970." Accordingly, The Middletown project was rushed to completion.

Until recently, Armco's voluntary program coincided very closely with mandated compliance. The water clarification plant for the Middletown hot strip mill came on stream in 1968. The demonstration plant for Best Available Technology (BAT), is, according to Barker, still considered the last word in water purification. The clarification system received the Civil Engineers Award of 1974, an honor usually reserved for bridges, dams, and other large public structures.

None of which means Armco is home free as far as water quality goes. "They stuck us with what they call EEQ [existing effluent quality]," explained Barker. "They said: 'This is the water quality you have today. This is what you're always going to have.' " The clarification plant was built to handle 100,000 gallons a minute, the combined water consumption of Cincinnati and Middletown. This capacity allowed for growth in strip production. "The plant is not yet up to full load. We're actually running [in 1977] at 76,000 gallons a minute." In other words, the plant has a bench mark that outlaws full utilization. "They have taken property from us," charged Barker. One of the gripes of Armco and others in all this is that little note is taken of past progress. No one calls Armco to ask why the river isn't red any more. All emphasis is on the very small problem remaining. Business argues that past progress disposed of 99 percent of the pollution. It's contended that capturing the remaining 1 percent will be prohibitively expensive.

U.S. Steel had spent $1 billion on cleanup through 1978. The cost of operating and maintaining control equipment was placed at $265 million a year. "And the end is nowhere in sight," said Roderick. "We're being forced to install equipment to control fugitive emissions at steelmaking locations and the costs of capturing that last one percent of pollution can be hundreds of times greater than what was spent to control 99 percent of the pollution associated with that same process." Fugitive emissions are the incidental particles that travel outside the main collection systems. They can be caused by charging or tapping furnaces. They can also arise from raw materials, piles, unpaved roads, or farm fields. To surround these stray wisps, large quantities of air must be filtered.

COUNTERPRODUCTIVITY OF EXTREME REGULATION

There is considerable doubt that the more stringent environmental measures produce any net benefit. The steel industry drew up a string of examples of requirements that meant net increases in pollution. "We have demonstrated that at specific locations," said Barker. "The Kansas City scarfing machine is one. To produce the electricity to run fans and motors to clean up the scarfing machines means that the local power plant would produce more pollution than we will capture."

The dimensions of the remaining problems are indicated by the difficulty of monitoring emissions. "We're talking numbers smaller than the analytical tools can detect," says

V. W. Foltz, who heads environmental research for Armco. "It seems kind of silly to be measuring fifty parts per million cyanide when the reliability is plus or minus 25. It sure looks as though all big problems have been cleaned up."

It's charged that the small room for improvement has produced a nit-picking style of regulation with little regard for the nominal objectives. One example is cited by Speer of U. S. Steel: "Last August, OSHA compliance officers arrived at our South Chicago works on the pretext of investigating three complaints. Instead they launched a plant-wide inspection that lasted for three months. They refused the daily requests of plant management to be informed of any observed violations—but waited six months to file a number of citations for alleged safety violations, and demanded that the plant correct many of them within 24 hours. Why did they investigate South Works, which is one of our safest plants, with a safety record last year that was twice as good as the overall record of our Central Steel Division? And if, indeed, there were unsafe acts committed in the plant, why did OSHA wait six months to call them to our attention? Perhaps, because their primary interest was not the safety of employees—but to impose a fine of more than $200,000."

Speer gives a second example: U. S. Steel's coal mines are being subjected to an average of 5,000 safety inspections every year. Each of these 5,000 inspections had an effect on production at the mine being inspected. "We estimate that productivity in our coal mines has decreased by 22 percent in the past four years—and one out of every four of those lost tons of production has been due to federal regulations and the interruptions caused by government safety inspections. Are those inspections necessary? Again, U. S. Steel's coal mine safety record is one of the best in the entire coal industry. During the past five years, the safety performance in our underground mines has averaged six times better than the

balance of the industry. And with this type of safety performance, it is difficult to understand why government safety
inspectors should be visiting our coal operations on the
average of twenty times a day, every working day of the year."

At one point, a U. S. Steel coal mine had a better safety
record than government offices. This mine may or may not
have been made a little safer because it was incessantly
inspected. What is certain is that it was made less productive.

The banning of dierrin, aldrin, and other pesticides may
have health benefits. There is a strong probability, however,
that these will be outweighed by what the *Wall Street Journal*
on August 15, 1978 called the "worst infestation of grasshop-
pers in twenty years. The summer of 1978 may well mark the
first major success of the radical fringe of the environmental
movement in giving the country back to the bugs."

The romanticizing of nature is all right up to a point. That
point is passed by those who insist every element in nature is
part of some grand, benevolent scheme. There is beauty in
virgin forests, but nature also produces such unpleasant
things as hurricanes, floods, and plagues. Vegetation produces the same ozone that is considered obnoxious when
emitted by factories.

In terms of beauty and known usefulness, many plants and
animals have to be classed as inconsequential. It is certainly
difficult to see why great importance should be attached to
the continued existence of the snail darter, a minnow-sized
fish which swims in the Little Tennessee River. Under the
Endangered Species Act of 1973, however, the Supreme
Court ruled that the river could not be dammed because it is
the home of the snail darter. A similar threat to the fur-
bish lousewart promised to halt construction of the
Dickey-Lincoln Dam on the St. John River in Maine.

Underlying all this is the notion that man is tampering
with a natural system that is extremely fragile and perish-

able. There is beauty in nature. There is also beauty in a nice home with well-tended lawns and gardens. It just isn't true that man spoils everything he touches, whereas nature is always kind and sweet.

All evidence suggests the free market is more effective than regulation in upgrading quality. This is true because the market provides control through an infinite number of very specific decisions and choices. No general regulation can possibly produce the right choice for a housewife in Peoria, a businessman in New York, and an airline pilot in Alaska. The regulators say advancing technology makes government control necessary. This may apply in a few very specialized areas, but as a general thing, the reverse is true. Central control is impossible because of the advance of technology and the growing complexity of the economy. "No one has the wisdom to manage the whole economy," said George Stinson, chairman of National Steel.

There doesn't seem much hope of convincing the Washington bureaucracy that they do not possess infinite wisdom. Given the realities of the times, the most that can be hoped for is the establishment of a system of priorities. The need to reduce the nation's vulnerability on energy is certainly of overriding importance. The goals of increasing fuel supplies and decreasing energy use should have dominant force in environmental, health, safety, and other areas. Any rule that works against expansion on the energy supply should be tabled until we are in a more comfortable position.

There is an urgent need to improve national productivity. This is one of the keys to checking inflation. We can't allow productive projects to be blocked by the regulators. The direct effect of regulation in causing inflation must be given greater consideration. In all areas, there must be a more intelligent evaluation of costs and benefits.

Chapter 7

GOVERNMENT SOCIAL SPENDING

Government spending in 1977, at all levels came to $621 billion. This number reflected government control of a growing share of national output. From 10 percent of Gross National Product in 1929, government spending rose to 19 percent in 1939 and to just under 33 percent in 1977. By subtracting huge sums, government is repressing the private economy. Not enough capital is left to modernize and expand industry. The tax bite is stifling effort and innovation. It may be contributing to serious erosion of freedom.

There is an urgent need to control government spending and to reduce taxes. The problem in this regard is that the big expansion of government is in the social area. The monies and benefits distributed by federal and local agencies in 1975 came to $286 million. Social spending accounted for nearly half the federal budget in 1977. Efforts to check the spending surge are challenged by the contention that government isn't doing enough, that the rich are too rich and the poor are too poor. Supporters of this view say more income should be distributed downward.

THE QUESTION OF INCOME TRANSFER

The question of income distribution must be addressed by anyone who proposes tax reductions. The most obscure changes in the tax code are invariably related to richness and poorness. When the capital gains tax reduction was put forward in 1978, President Carter said the cut would mean

TABLE 7-1. Composition of Budget Outlays by Fiscal Years

	1967	1974	1977	1978 (est.)	1979 (est.)
		In billions of dollars			
National defense	$ 68.2	$ 77.8	$ 97.5	$107.6	$117.8
Payments for individuals	40.1	111.1	181.7	196.9	214.5
Net interest	10.3	21.5	30.0	35.2	39.9
All other	39.7	59.3	92.7	122.4	128.0
Total	158.3	269.6	401.9	462.2	500.2
		Percentage distribution			
National defense	43.1	28.8	24.3	23.3	23.6
Payments for individuals	25.3	41.2	45.2	42.6	42.9
Net interest	6.5	8.0	7.5	7.6	8.0
All other	25.1	22.0	23.1	26.5	25.6
Total	100.0	100.0	100.0	100.0	100.0
		As a percentage of GNP			
National defense	8.8	5.7	5.3	5.3	5.2
Payments for individuals	5.2	8.2	9.9	9.6	9.4
Net interest	1.3	1.6	1.6	1.7	1.8
All other	5.1	4.3	5.0	6.0	5.6
Total	20.4	19.8	21.9	22.6	22.0

Source: The Budget of the United States Government, Fiscal Year 1979.

"huge windfalls for millionaires and two bits for the average citizen." New social programs are advanced with the promise that they will be paid for by closing tax loopholes and soaking the rich.

Until recently, the basic issues were skirted by those who opposed further redistribution. Business taxes should be cut because business needed more money, and there should be tax cuts for those who save and invest in business. That isn't enough today. "Corporations don't pay taxes," said Roger Herriott of the Census Bureau. "People do." His point was that company taxes as well as individual taxes ultimately come out of the incomes of people.

In the absence of a full airing, the images emerging were those of enlightened humanitarianism on the side of government social spending and self-seeking reaction on the other. In the last few years, however, the case against income transfer has been taken up by two groups with special credentials. In California and elsewhere, middle-income people have spoken with great force against high taxes. It can no longer be maintained that the status quo is defended only by a handful of the super-rich.

Equally interesting have been defections from the egalitarian movement in the academic community. A number of highly educated economists have made detailed examinations of what is now being done to redistribute income, and the philosophical implications of transfer have been analyzed. One general conclusion is that the enormous sums now being transferred are enough to eliminate poverty, as will be explained in this chapter. A second point is that attempts to increase the re-distributed share will produce numerous negative effects—including a reduction in the amount available for redistribution.

In addition to shedding new light on the subject of redistribution, the educators have given intellectual respectability to the cause of holding down taxes. The pros and cons of the matter were argued in 1977 at a forum staged by the American Enterprise Institute for Public Policy (AEI) and the Hoover Institution on War, Revolution, and Peace.

Compiled by AEI in a book called *Income Redistribution: Proceedings of a Conference Held in Washington, May 1976,* the arguments against further redistribution were as scholarly as those in favor. That is not to say most intellectuals now favor limits on income transfer; one complaint is that egalitarianism is being imposed by a small group made up in large part by academic people. But, for what it's worth, the case for inequality of income distribution can no longer be represented as propaganda from dull-witted businessmen.

Among other findings, the new probings have identified a change in the character of income transfer. The current view in liberal circles is indicated by a passage from the Brookings Institution report of George F. Break and Joseph Pechman.[1] "The primary goal of taxation," wrote the authors, "is to transfer control of resources from one group in the society to another and to do so in ways that do not jeopardize . . . the attainment of other economic goals." This statement may come as a surprise to many people. The Constitution was never amended to give government the job of redistributing income, said Senator S. I. Hayakawa (R., Calif.). "That, however, is the principal function of our government today," he says in the July, 1978, *Readers Digest.*

The implications of all this are profound. It is now supposedly up to government to control the degree of economic equality in the country. Taxation has long had an effect on income distribution: it has long been accepted that rich people should pay more taxes than poor people. What is now being claimed, however, is a formal, specific right of government to use taxes in shaping the income structure. The distinction between this kind of government operation and a socialist government is extremely thin. There are those who feel that we are, indeed, heading toward a basic change in our form of government.

WHO GETS WHAT?

In 1975, no federal income taxes were paid by 230 individuals with incomes over $200,000. This statistic always gets good play in the papers. Not mentioned is the fact that taxes were paid by the other 34,000 or so in the top bracket. What's needed is a complete picture of incomes and taxes. How rich are the rich? How high are their taxes? How widespread is poverty, and what is being done to help the poor?

Since answers to these questions are basic to the whole issue of national income distribution, it might be expected that a clear assembly of facts would be available, but that isn't the case. Given the best intentions, it is difficult to find out who is getting what. If someone is out to make a point, convenient sets of figures are readily available to corroborate just about any claim. "The income distribution can be made to look soothingly equal or shockingly unequal, depending on how the figures are lined up," said Arthur Okun.[2] When income transfers are factored in, the potential for confusion is unlimited. "By selectively considering only some of the hundreds of government programs, it is possible to make almost any position sound plausible," said Edgar Browning, "—that the system is pro-poor, pro-rich, pro-middle class, pro-black. . . .[3]

There are varied bundles of information to choose from. More important, however, the basic Census Bureau numbers are wrong—or, at least, incomplete. The wrongness went undetected until it occurred to a few people that the amount of income reported didn't correspond with the income available. More specifically, the amount of poverty was out of line with the amount being spent to relieve poverty. In an October 13, 1978 editorial, the *Wall Street Journal* contrasted statistics on the reduction in poverty with the increase in transfer payments in a recent period. "Are we really to believe that only 11 million persons were raised from poverty with an expenditure of $129 billion—$11,727 a head?" asked the *Journal.* A discrepancy was indicated earlier in a study by the Census Bureau team of Roger Herriott and Herman Miller. In one of the few really comprehensive analyses, the two men sorted out not only transfer payments but all forms of income. Things like capital gains and retained corporate earnings were taken into account in calculating the incomes of individuals. Corporate income taxes and corporate property taxes were likewise allotted to people. When these additions were made, there were considerably more wealthy people and considerably fewer poor people than the official figures showed: in 1968 there were actually 900,000 families or individuals with incomes over $50,000 a year; that compared with the official tally of 200,000. In the same year, there were about ten million families with incomes under $3,000 a year. That was two million less than the number reported in the official census.

The Miller-Herriott studies showed disproportionate income shares at the top and the bottom. Over 16 percent of all families were in the under $3,000 class. This group had 2 percent of all income. Eleven percent of all income went to the 1.4 percent with incomes over $50,000. In the middle sector—from $7,000 to $50,000—the income share was in line with population. Just under 60 percent of all families were in this bracket, and they received just over 60 percent of all income.

All this suggests that the million families with very high incomes should share some of their excess with the ten million who have very little, and the federal tax structure is designed to promote this exchange. "Federal taxes as a whole are roughly proportional in the middle income ranges and are sharply progressive in the upper levels," said the Census team. Since federal taxes account for 56 percent of all taxes, this pattern applies to some extent to the whole picture. The total structure is highly progressive at the upper end. Despite the headlines about millionaires who get off scot-free, the total tax rate on incomes over $50,000 was 45 percent in 1968. Nearly half of all taxes in 1968 were paid by the highest fifth on the income register. Those in the top 5 percent paid nearly a fourth of all taxes.

State and local taxes tend to be nonprogressive. In the lower brackets, this is enough to make the whole structure lopsided. If income transfers are neglected, the total tax rate in 1968 was 50 percent for those with incomes under $2,000, as table 7-2 shows. The tax rate increased from the middle-income to the lower-income brackets. When an adjustment was made to include transfers on which taxes were paid, the tax rate for the under-$2,000 group fell to 26 percent. When income was adjusted to include all benefits received from the government, the rate for the same group was −56 percent. For those in the $2,000-to-$3,000 bracket, the rate was −14 percent in 1968. "In other words," said Roger Herriott, "those with incomes under $2,000 received $3.5 billion more in transfers than they paid in taxes."

This point is not recognized, because the official Census Bureau figures don't include the nonmoney portions of government transfers. "They don't show up," says Herriott. "These kinds of things are not in their figures." There has been no comparable Census study since 1968, but it is Herriott's opinion that the impact of nonmoney transfers is considerably greater today than it was in that year.

An extremely important disclosure of the Herriott-Miller

studies was the manner in which the tax-transfer structure is rigged against work in the low-income brackets. A man is heavily taxed if he works; he receives hefty benefits if he doesn't work.

The effect of this bias was examined by Martin Feldstein of Harvard in an example based on Massachusetts provisions. "The combination of taxes and unemployment compensation imposes as effective marginal tax rate of 81 percent—that is, the man's net earnings fall by only 19 percent of his gross pay when he is unemployed for ten weeks. For a wide variety of representative unemployed men in the nation, the compensation benefits replace more than 60 percent of the lost net income. In the more generous states, the replacement of net earnings is generally over 80 percent."[4]

TABLE 7-2. Government Tax and Transfer Rates as a Percentage of Total Income—1968

ADJUSTED MONEY INCOME LEVELS	TAXES	GOVERNMENT TRANSFER PAYMENTS	TAXES MINUS TRANSFER PAYMENTS
Under $2,000	50.0	106.5	−56.5
2,000–4,000	34.6	48.5	−13.9
4,000–6,000	31.0	19.6	11.4
6,000–8,000	30.1	8.6	21.5
8,000–10,000	28.2	5.5	23.7
10,000–15,000	29.8	3.9	25.9
15,000–25,000	30.0	3.0	27.0
25,000–50,000	32.8	2.1	30.7
50,000 plus	45.0	0.4	44.7
Total tax and transfer rates	31.6	6.9	24.6

Source: Roger Herriott and Herman Miller, "The Taxes We Pay," *Conference Board Record,* May 1971.

POVERTY CONTINUES

The Census study attracted some attention, but the findings on transfers were part of a long report. The meaning of the transfer estimates didn't really register. It was not until 1975 that the subject received a full airing in the AEI study by Edgar K. Browning of the University of Virginia. Browning focused squarely on the subject of income transfer. Like others since then, he could not understand why the sharp increase in social spending had not had more effect in reducing poverty and changing income shares. According to his calculations, the amount transferred rose from $88 billion in 1966 to $212 billion in 1973.

His studies, summarized in table 7-3, showed that about half the total transfer—$100 billion—went to those in the lowest quarter of the income scale. He subtracted the $22.5 billion tax payment of this group and came up with a net transfer of $77.5 billion. He deducted $11.8 billion in education spending and arrived at a final transfer of $65.7 billion. That averaged out to $1,248 for every person in the poorest fourth of the nation. Adding pre-transfer income of $564 a person, the average total income was $1,810 a person or $7,240 for a family of four. The official poverty line for a family of four was $4,540 in 1973. Browning concluded that enough money was being spent to lift everyone out of extreme poverty. When a full count was made, he said, the lowest fifth had 8 percent of all income in 1973. The official figure that year was 5.5 percent.

In discussing the contradictory numbers, Browning said there could be only one answer: "The most important explanation by far is that a large fraction of the total transfer is not counted as income at all. Government statistics on the money incomes of low-income families are totally unreliable as a measure of the real incomes of these families."

The Census Bureau freely acknowledges the limitations of its data. Income statistics are compiled by going out and asking people how much money they make or receive. The numbers for 1975 were assembled by sending interviewers to about 150 million housing units. "Money income does not reflect the fact that some families receive part of their income in the form of nonmoney transfers such as food stamps, health benefits, and subsidized housing," said the Census Bureau.

According to Browning, this is precisely the area that has seen the greatest rise in downward transfers. From $1.5 million in 1964, federal nonmoney transfers to those in the

TABLE 7-3.   Social Welfare Benefits to the Lowest Fourth of Incomes

	1960	1966	1973
Total social welfare ($ billions)	51.4	87.6	214.6
Percentage transferred to lowest fourth	44%	43%	47%
Gross transfer ($ billions)	22.8	37.6	100.7
Taxes paid ($ billions)	8.4	12.5	22.5
Net transfer ($ billions)	14.4	25.1	78.2
Education ($ billions)	3.2	5.9	11.8
Net transfer (excl. educ.) ($ billions)	11.2	19.2	66.4
Net transfer (excl. educ.) per capita (dollars)	247	387	1,248
Net income (excl. educ.) per capita (dollars)	603	845	1,812
Net transfer (excl. educ.) as a percentage of net income	41%	46%	69%

Source: Edgar K. Browning, *Redistribution and the Welfare System,* Washington, D.C.: American Enterprise Institute, 1975. Copyright © 1978 by American Enterprise Institute.

poverty bracket rose to $15.1 billion in 1973. The in-kind transfers were less than 20 percent of the total in 1964. They were 58 percent of a much larger total in 1973. Browning estimated that 40 percent of the transfers to the entire bottom fourth were in nonmoney form. In addition, he figured that state and local transfers to the poverty sector were $7.5 billion in 1973, with half of this in nonmoney form. "That 23 million people were officially regarded as poor in 1973 was not due to a lack of resources, but rather to the fact that $18.8 billion of in-kind transfers were not counted as income," he points out.

It's also probable that cash transfers are understated. "It has been determined," says the Census Bureau, "that wages and salaries tend to be much better reported than such income types as public assistance, Social Security, and net income from interest, dividends and rents." The Bureau makes some guesses about the amount of unreported income, but of the $126 billion estimated for 1975, about 90 percent was assigned to dividends, interest, and the like. The amounts added to the various transfer payments were relatively minor.

The Congressional Budget Office analyzed the effect of the transfers in 1976, with results as seen in figure 7-1. Before taxes and before any transfers, more than 21 million families were below the poverty line. After cash transfers, the number was reduced to 10.7 million. After both money and non-money transfers, the number was down to 6.4 million (with Medicare and Medicaid figured in). There was a slight upward adjustment—to 6.6 million after the tax payments of poor people were netted out.

Like Browning, the Congressional Office noted the discrepancy between the amount of social spending and the results. From 1965 to 1975, a fourfold rise in spending supposedly reduced the percentage of families in poverty by only 30 percent. However, the inclusion of all transfers showed a much more dramatic change: "If income is looked at after taxes and after total transfers, the incidence of poverty among families has fallen by approximately 56 percent since 1965." Also like Browning, the Congressional staff observed that in-kind transfers made up a large portion of the total distributed downward.

All this is more than a statistical game. The important fact is that enough money is available to eliminate poverty and near poverty. "In 1973," said Arthur Okun, "four million American families with heads under 65 were living on incomes

FIGURE 7-1. Effect of Income Transfers on Poverty

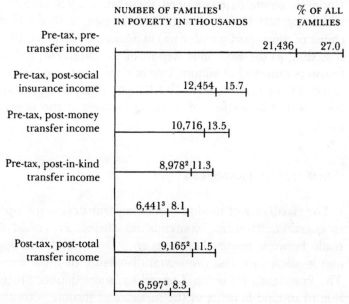

	NUMBER OF FAMILIES[1] IN POVERTY IN THOUSANDS	% OF ALL FAMILIES
Pre-tax, pre-transfer income	21,436	27.0
Pre-tax, post-social insurance income	12,454	15.7
Pre-tax, post-money transfer income	10,716	13.5
Pre-tax, post-in-kind transfer income	8,978[2]	11.3
	6,441[3]	8.1
Post-tax, post-total transfer income	9,165[2]	11.5
	6,597[3]	8.3

[1]Unrelated individuals are included as one-person families.
[2]Excludes Medicare and Medicaid benefits.
[3]Includes Medicare and Medicaid benefits.

Source: Congressional Budget Office, June 1977.

below the poverty level. Yet, the total shortfall in annual income below the poverty line for all people under 65 is only $9 billion. About nine million families with heads under 65 have incomes below the criterion of deprivation ($7,000). Yet, the aggregate shortfall of income below that line is only about $25 billion."

With government social spending in 1975 over $286 billion, it is incredible that poverty continues. Granted that more than half the total outlay went to programs not based on need. According to the Congressional study, 68 percent of the 1975 spending went to Social Security, unemployment compensation, and disability programs. But a third of that 68 percent went to families in the lowest 20 percent of the income series. Under programs based on need, these families got half of the remaining $94 billion. The problem, again, is that a large chunk of downward transfer was in nonmoney form. In 1977, according to the Economic Report of the president, in-kind transfers came to $43 billion. Two of these items, food stamps and child nutrition, came to $8.5 billion. That almost equaled the shortfall of income of working families in the poverty group.

NONMONEY TRANSFERS

The classifying of in-kind nonmoney transfers is still open to question. Browning contends no distinction should be made between money payments to provide food, housing, and medical care and the actual disbursing of these items. The President's Economic Council has some doubts. "Inclusion of in-kind benefits in the measure of income is controversial and almost certainly overstates the value of such transfers to recipients. Recipients have been found to value cash more highly than in-kind benefits because it affords greater freedom of choice. . . . Nevertheless," the Council adds, "it would be inappropriate to ignore such benefits [as medicare] in a comprehensive measure of income." It might be very inappropriate, but it is still important to note the difference between cash and noncash benefits. As the Council indicates, nonmoney transfers give government the power to determine what goods and services will be made available. One authority offers a half-hearted defense of this practice, saying it protects poor people from competition in the free market. This is nonsense.

The protection is unwarranted and bitterly resented, says Thomas Sowell, of the Center for Advanced Study in Behavioral Sciences at Stamford. Described as a black conservative, Sowell has caustic words for the substitution of goods for money. "Central to the costly 'caretaker' approach to helping the poor—by paying money to someone else—is an image of the poor as too helpless to make it with mere money. "The image of helplessness of the poor is repeatedly invoked to defeat proposals for income maintenance, educational vouchers, and any other reforms that would enable the poor to make their own decisions." In rejecting this image, Sowell cites the massive emigration of blacks from the South in the last two generations. "This was a spontaneous decision of millions of individuals not organized by indigenous leaders."[5]

The poor are not alone in having choices made for them in government. About half the transfer payments move laterally. Government taxes people and sends money or benefits back to people. For that percentage of the transfer in cash form, the main objection is the waste involved in the roundabout movement of income. Medicare and various miscellaneous programs disburse nonmoney benefits in the upper brackets. In one affluent New Jersey area, $800,000 was spent in a recent year to provide free bus service for kids living within a two-mile radius of the school. Nobody turns down a free ride, however unnecessary. But the ride isn't really free: someone has mandated that the taxpayers will spend part of their income on school transportation. If there were a choice, there would doubtless be a lot of kids walking to the New Jersey school.

In other areas, the wisdom of the choices mandated by government is very much open to question. "There is general agreement among students of the economics of health care that Medicare and Medicaid ignited an explosion of health care costs," said Martin Feldstein. "Today, patients over age 65 pay more out of pocket for medical care than they did a decade ago before the beginning of Medicare." Feldstein refers to "the bloated demand for expensive services of physicans and hospitals for minor conditions."

As Thomas Sowell suggests, the thread running through much of the social spending effort—and government regulation—is that people aren't wise enough to choose for themselves. (Incidentally, Edgar Browning gives figures showing that poor people spend smaller percentages of their incomes for alcohol and recreation than rich people.) The implication that people need shielding from unfettered free markets is derided by Irving Kristol of New York University. Far from frustrating the poor, says Kristol, the market is highly responsive to the wants of people. He sees this response as a source of consumerist hostility toward business. "The attack on the large corporation is an elitist attack on an organization that is too democratic," he says.

ADMINISTRATIVE COSTS

There is another argument against nonmoney transfers and, to some extent, against all transfers. That is the ineffi- ciency that goes with having a middleman involved. In much of this whole discussion, it has been assumed that the discrepancy between money spent and money received is accounted for by underreporting. Another explanation could be that poor people simply aren't receiving all the money supposedly disbursed. A certain amount is unquestionably soaked up in the administrative chain. It was recently reported that $7 billion had gone astray in the Department of Health, Education, and Welfare.

In addition, there are inherent inequities in many of the welfare programs. The second biggest welfare program, Aid to Families with Dependent Children, primarily benefits female-headed households. The biggest welfare program, Medicaid, doesn't help people who are not sick. Veterans pensions, housing assistance, and other transfers have selective, limited beneficiaries. In short, the averages don't reflect the actual receipts of all low-income people. There is a concentration in the hands of some and neglect of others.

As to the amount of leakage in the transfer process, there are cynical comments from Thomas Sowell: "Obviously, there are a lot of middlemen who get theirs," wrote Sowell. "Such caretakers are the modern equivalent of the missionaries who came to do good and stayed do well. Poverty is the cause of much affluence." But the administrative costs of the big transfer programs don't appear to be excessive. For Social Security (Old Age and Survivors Insurance Trust Fund), the administrative expense was 1.4 percent of benefit payments in 1977. In the same year, administration of the disability fund took an amount equal to 3.4 percent of benefit payments (1978 annual report of the Fedral Old Age and Survivors Insurance and Disability Funds).

I would assume it takes more administration for something like public housing than for mailing checks to retired people. The Economic Council makes this general comment: "The welfare system is both inefficient and exceedingly complex.

141

Administrative expenses account for large portions of the total budgets for the various programs, and the error rates are high." The problem with welfare administration is not just the cost but the fact that it provides a constituency for continued complexity and steady expansion of social spending.

What's needed, it seems to me, is some kind of simplified, consolidated cash program. As both Sowell and the Economic Council note, welfare recipients would prefer cash on the barrel head. One proposal calls for income below a certain level to be considered negative for tax purposes. Edgar Browning favors a negative income tax (NIT), but he cautions this could not be imposed on top of the programs now in existence. He also cautions that replacing these programs will be difficult: "Any attempt to substitute an NIT for the present system would encounter tough political resistance, because of the broad range of special interest groups that obtain substantial advantages under the current array of policies. One of these groups, usually not thought of as such, is strategically situated: the government employees who administer the current 168 federal programs . . . . This group may well constitute the greatest obstacle to meaningful reform of the welfare system."

The idea of a negative tax is not all that novel, says Browning. Food stamps and Medicaid are really negative taxes; they are benefits distributed to those below prescribed income levels. The Earned Income Tax Credit, enacted in 1975 and enlarged in 1978, formalized the negative tax concept.

The Carter administration has proposed consolidation of three programs: food stamps, supplemental income for the blind, and the federal share of Aid to Families with Dependent Children. These would be replaced by a single cash assistance program. There would be two tiers: higher benefits would go to the blind and others not expected to work; smaller payments would be received by two-parent families and others expected to find work. These would be steps in the right direction.

THE EFFECT OF TAX RATES

With more efficient distribution and with better reporting, hopefully there will come a time when the elimination of extreme poverty is a reality. Assuming this happens, it doesn't necessarily follow that nothing should be done about the richness of the rich. There is still the question of why some people should receive a great deal more than other people. Shouldn't the rich be made to give some of their excess to the poor?

One major consideration is that the rich are already being soaked by the tax collector. The Herriott-Miller studies showed that nearly half the income of rich people went to taxes. (By 1974, those with adjusted gross incomes over $100,000 paid an average of more than $66,000 in taxes.) It seems elementary that government should not take more of any income than the individual gets. Arthur Okun, who believes there should be greater redistribution, acknowledges there is a hefty subtraction from the high-income brackets: "The rich and the super-rich do pay proportionately more taxes than the average American. In 1972, that top group with incomes above $50,000 paid $22 billion in federal personal income taxes. The progressive part (that in excess of the 11 percent national average tax) amounted to $13 billion—more than the total federal cost of Medicaid, welfare, food stamps, and public housing combined."[6]

The other major consideration is the amount available from soaking the rich. There is a tendency for government to promise great things if tax loopholes for the rich are closed. "Tax reform can provide dollars for homes and health and education," said Senator Edward Kennedy (D., Mass.). "Clearly, when we talk about tax reform, we are not talking about insignificant amounts." These notions are derided by Elsie Waters of the Tax Formation. "It's the oldest political scheme in the world to tell people the government isn't doing enough and someone else should pay for it."

Irving Kristol has observed that redistribution is a futile policy for the developing nations, because there isn't enough extra wealth to do any good. It turns out our own situation is not dissimilar. "If the maximum annual salary were set at $60,000," said Arthur Okun, "the total amount saved would be only a fraction of one percent of the national wage bill."

The returns would also be negligible if the ceiling were imposed by raising taxes instead of lowering salaries. "In 1970," said Edgar Browning, "the total adjusted gross income [AGI] . . . for taxpayers with AGI above $100,00 was $14.4 billion. An increase in their tax rates from one-half to two-thirds would raise only $2 billion. . . . What these facts make clear is that taxing the wealthy very heavily will not permit a significant lightening of the burden for the remainder of the population."[7] Browning's point was that added redistribution means soaking the middle class as well as the rich. All the evidence suggests such broad taxation would be self-defeating in terms of the amount of income transferred.

When the Nixon Game Plan applied tax restraints in 1969, federal revenues showed no change in 1970 and declined in 1971. By way of contrast, the Kennedy tax cuts in 1962 and 1964 were followed by sharp increases in federal revenues.

These responses were not accidental, in the opinion of Arthur B. Laffer, an economist at the University of Southern California. The Laffer Curve, described in Chapter 1, depicts the effect of tax changes on tax revenues. At low levels, lifting the tax rate brings in more money. At some higher level, the repressive effect of a tax increase reduces government revenues. Laffer believes U. S. taxes have reached the point of diminishing returns.

Despite this, tax planners continue to act as though they were dealing with a frozen economy. "In 1969," said Congressman Steiger "the Treasury Department estimated that capital gains revenues would increase if the maximum rates were increased. Revenues declined almost 40 percent in the first year." In 1978, Steiger's proposal for a cut in capital gains taxes was opposed on the grounds that it would reduce revenues. "The static analysis shows a revenue loss of $2.4 billion. It is based on the unrealistic assumption that nothing will happen in the financial world."

Something does happen when tax rates are changed. The sensitivity of the economy to tax changes is one of the most important facts to emerge from recent ups and downs. The economic repression flowing from higher tax rates tends to reduce total tax revenues.

THE SAVINGS RATE

In Martin Feldstein's words, "The most serious effect of our Social Security program is to reduce the nation's rate of savings and therefore our rate of capital accumulation." Feldstein's thought is that the Social Security system reduces the need for the individual to save for his future. In terms of capital supply, the system doesn't replace individual savings, because it operates on a pay-as-you-go basis. On the other had, Nancy Teeters of the Federal Reserve argued that Social Security really increased savings. "Without Social Security, I would be contributing to the support of my mother, my mother-in-law, and quite possibly, my aunt, and that would depress my savings rate."

Not directly related to income transfer is the build-up of private pension funds. According to one estimate, these now equal about 25 percent of the average company's assets. To some extent, the funds represent mandated savings. The government now specifies the amount to be accumulated to meet a given obligation.

Whether the funds replace or supplement individual savings is anybody's guess. By contributing to the instability of common stock prices, the funds have probably tended to drive individual investors out of the stock market. Whatever the effect, there is no question that both union demands and government rules are channeling huge sums into funds for deferred compensation.

Arthur Okun thinks people are fussing too much over the savings rate. "Goldsmith, Kuznets, and Denison have told us that for periods going back to 1870, we have had a very steady national and personal saving rate." Okun doubts that it is necessary or desirable to increase this rate. In proposing 33-percent tax cuts, Jack Kemp said the findings cited by Okun are rejected by many modern economists. "They feel strongly that saving can be increased, and should be increased, and government policy, including tax policy, can have a strong impact on saving."

As to why savings should be increased, the Kemp-Roth thesis was that the way to make the economy grow was to boost supply. Supply could be expanded only if people could save more money and had an incentive to invest in projects that promoted growth. A second reason for a higher savings rate is the need to finance federal deficits. Jack Kemp said stimulative effects of his tax cut would reduce or eliminate the deficits. At the same time, the enlarged capital pool would enable the government to borrow without creating a credit squeeze.

THE INCENTIVE TO WORK

Apart from broad economic effects, there is the question of how income transfer affects the behavior of people. There is then the question of whether or not any adverse effects are serious enough to make further redistribution undesirable. It's generally accepted that efficiency and output do suffer when income is taken from some people and given to others. Even those who favor further redistribution acknowledge that there is a trade-off and that this limits the amount of income transfer.

Full income equality would have too high a cost in reduced efficiency and growth, Arthur Okun indicated, in the *New York Times Magazine* (July 4, 1976), "For the vast majority, an equal slice of a shrunken pie would be unacceptable. If, for example, full equality of income costs us a generation's worth of growth (an optimistic guess in my judgment), four-fifths of our citizens would be made worse by that trade." Similar comments come from James Tobin of Yale in AEI's *Income Redistribution:* "One must reason some compromise between the desirability of moving toward less inequality and the loss of social efficiency that results."

Okun uses the expression "leaky bucket" to describe the losses that result from tax and transfer programs, and among those losses were administrative and compliance costs, misplaced work efforts resulting from them, and "distortion of innovative behavior as well as saving and investment behavior." He argues that there could be greater redistribution without such great losses in these areas. Jack Kemp and many others see a need to restore incentive to workers, savers, and investors in America. Arthur Laffer was quoted by Associated Press along the same lines. "People don't work to pay taxes; they work for what they get after taxes," said Laffer. "If you lower taxes, you make the activity more profitable for the doer of the activity."

Others agree that worker incentives are crucial and that people do respond to monetary incentives. "I believe that our extensive program of social insurance has had important effects on the economy," said Martin Feldstein in *Income Redistribution*. "There is little room for doubt that our current system of unemployment compensation increases the rate and duration of unemployment." Feldstein cited estimates that jobless pay extends unemployment spans more than 30 percent. His own earlier guess was that unemployment compensation contributed 1.25 percent to the permanent jobless rate.

The experience of industry makes it clear that the urge to work is affected by the generosity of jobless payments. When contracts call for state compensation to be supplemented by company funds, there have been union demands that senior people be given the right to be laid off first. This is a fundamental change in the whole notion of seniority. Feldstein cautioned that negative income tax plans, which could guarantee a minimum income, could bring significant subtractions from the work force. The problem of dropouts could become critical in coming years. Population experts say we are approaching a time when abnormally heavy retirements will coincide with abnormally light additions to the work force.

THE SQUEEZED MIDDLE CLASS MAJORITY

In the opinion of many, all the adverse effects of greater redistribution would be outweighed by the good effects; it's argued that more equality is so desirable it's worth the sacrifice of some growth and efficiency. Arthur Okun noted that people are given equal rights in the areas of voting, free speech and access to public services, and that equality should apply in the economic realm as well. Professor John Rawls of Harvard also relied on popular judgment in establishing the case for equality. In his book *A Theory of Justice*, Rawls asserts that if they didn't know what slots they would occupy, people would choose a society in which all values were distributed equally.

It may well be the "original position" of Rawls would produce the judgment he predicts. It is probably true that the general idea of equality has considerable attractiveness to most people. But it was not true that toward the end of the twentieth century there was a mass verdict in favor of greater redistribution. Events of 1978 made it crystal clear most people feel they are being made worse by taxation. The popular mood was indicated by support for the Kemp-Roth bill and for the Steiger capital gains proposal. The California vote on Proposition 13 was an explicit protest against excessive taxation. In that instance the consequences of the tax cut were spelled out in advance: there would have to be cuts in "vital services." It turned out most voting people considered themselves the sponsors rather than the beneficiaries of such services and felt they would benefit more from less government spending and greater reliance on the private, unequal system. And the size of the California vote showed that this belief was not confined to a handful of the super-rich. "It is by no means clear that the affluent have, in fact, predominated in opposing increased public spending in these areas," said

Walter J. Blum of the University of Chicago, another *Income Redistribution* writer, "On balance, the middle class has been the most cautious about moves to initiate or expand programs requiring new government expenditures."

There is one obvious reason for this to be true. Increased government spending has to mean higher taxes for middle-income people. These people can't afford to pay more and maintain their standard of living and saving. They are in a no-man's land between the rich and the poor: they are excluded from the scholarships, the food stamps, and other benefits of low-income people; they don't have the abundance that allows the rich to pay without privation. As Irving Kristol has noted, most people are now in the middle class. Policies that would worsen the lives of most people have to be considered unacceptable.

THE GROUNDS FOR INCOME EQUALITY

Majority rule notwithstanding, the case for income equality is argued on the grounds that the existing inequality has no clear basis in merit. If merit is defined strictly as effort, it may be true that a company laborer is exerting himself more than the company president. There is no way of knowing this is not so as a general thing, said Yale's James Tobin in *Income Redistribution*. "We have a great stake in maintaining the view that performance pays off, that indolence and inefficiency do not," said Tobin. "Since we cannot disentangle the elements of endowment and effort in performance, we must tolerate considerable reward for endowment, in large measure undeserved and redundant." It is certainly true that some people are born with greater potentials than others; however, these are only potentials—they can be developed or dissipated.

Without the prospect of rewards, there would be a great deal more dissipation than development.

Blum makes the point that with economic equality, inequality among people would be based to a large extent on natural endowments. A person's status would be determined on the basis of beauty, strength, personality, and so forth. As it is, a dull, ugly person can be successful through sheer effort. And while the exact contribution can't be measured, it can be assumed that effort is an important element in progress.

The question of merit comes up in another sense. The ill-gotten gains of the rich should be redistributed because they were derived from the sufferings and repression of the masses. In the days of sweatshops and child labor, there might have been some substance to this contention. Today, there are labor unions and minimum wage laws, there is an Occupational Safety and Health Administration, and there is a competitive system that forces owners to turn over most of a company's output to consumers.

The case for equality has been argued on aesthetic grounds, namely that cultivated sensibilities are offended by the sight of people crawling in the gutter. The strongest case for equality rests on the morality of altruistic impulses and actions. Perfect conformance to the ideal of brotherly love would probably mean perfect equality. The ideal can't be disregarded—it stands at the top of the moral scale—but there are other considerations and values. There is the desire of individuals for material well-being, and there is the desirability of material progress for the nation as a whole. Given the imperfections of man and given the uneven distribution of talents, the best practical system must fall well short of full equality.

The imperfections of man mean that excessive taxation makes for corruption. The maximum federal income tax is now 70 percent. Milton Friedman estimated that a maximum rate of 25 percent in 1972 would have turned up six times more people with incomes over $500,000 a year than were actually reported.[8] If this estimate is correct, a great many rich people are finding ways to dodge taxes. There is much agitation over loopholes and shelters, but it may be too much to expect that men smart enough and aggressive enough to earn $500,000 will ever hand over 70 percent of their pay to the government. It is sad, perhaps, but true that aggressiveness leading to inequality is built into man's nature.

Finally, it may not be true, as Rawls contends, that people would choose equality if they did not know where they would land. The chancy nature of the system has an appeal that is brought out by the fondness of many people for gambling. "I think there is also some pleasure in the game of competing for a higher share in the distribution of income," said J. Carter Murphy of Southern Methodist University in *Income Redistribution*.

COERCION AND EQUALITY

Left to their own devices, people will arrange themselves at different unequal levels; it follows, then, that equality can be achieved only if some force alters the natural order. The fear is that the alteration now proposed through increased redistribution involves the suppression of liberty by the government. There are a number of reasons for taking this fear seriously. The magnitude of the equalizing effort is already monumental, and there is a change in the character of this effort. A prescribed economic order is now the starting point for income transfer. Inherent in this approach is repression and control. Government decides how much will be left to one person and how much will be given to another. The mechanics of taking money from one person and giving to another add to the size and power of government, and this expansion of government tends in turn to diminish the sector in which free, private activity is possible.

All this adds impetus to a regulatory build-up which is rapidly advancing. Regulation of income ties in with the tendency of government to regulate all aspects of behavior. Already in place is a large bureaucracy, eager to impose its wisdom on the masses.

Robert Nisbet of Columbia University is foremost among those who see a change in the nature of income transfer and social spending. Writing in AEI's *Income Redistribution*, he said, "I take the time-honored phrase, equality of opportunity, to mean, basically, equality of access to the law, to the rights and privileges and freedoms guaranted by law," said Nisbet. Today, however, equality of opportunity had become subtly fused with equality of result or condition."

If the result is predetermined, suggests Robert Nozick of Harvard in *Income Redistribution*, the method of reaching this result is also established. Government must intervene. Nozick does not like the method implied by this sequence. There should be "no judgment about the resulting distribution which would introduce the coercive arm of the state." The absence of coercion does not rule out redistribution, said Nozick. "If we do not like what it produces, we could choose to transfer some of our resources to rectify it by philanthropy." It's argued that what is really involved is a change in our form of government. "Equality and redistribution are code words for economic and social reconstuction that are revolutionary in character," said Nisbet.

Cited in this connection are sayings of wise men from other days. "Law-givers or revolutionaries who propose equality and liberty at the same time are either utopian dreamers or charlatans," said Goethe. Tocqueville saw the same incompatibility. In *Democracy in America* he wrote, "Every central power that follows its own natural tendencies courts and encourages the principle of equality. For equality singularly facilitates, extends, and secures the influence of the central power."

In the current situation, further redistribution has to have an element of coercion. Most people don't want more of their income transferred. This is not the old-fashioned griping about taxes. There is a specific protest against having money taken for social spending. "My guess is the great majority of American people share this view of the dangers inhering in any policy of large scale redistribution, of legislated equality," said Nisbet. The push for equality is coming from what Nisbet calls a small "clerisy" of intellectuals, politicians, and bureaucrats. It has been observed that this group is not motivated entirely by broad good will. Robert Novak referred to the "loathing" of some liberals for the silent majority. Nisbet in the AEI book noted the traditional contempt of radicals for the bourgeois. In some part, the push for equality reflects a fondness for the apparatus rather than the result. "As great as ever, I fear," said Nisbet, "is clerisy's preference for the public over the private, the big over the small."

The untidiness of the free market offends the academic mind. Still felt are attitudes formed by the failure of the free system in the Thirties. It certainly went against all reason to have ten years in which men and machines sat idle while people were in desperate need of goods and services. In theory, socialism offers a neat solution to depressions as well as to inequality. If the economic workings of the system are distrusted, there is equal distrust for qualitative results. . Educators and bureaucrats see private enterprise and free markets producing environmental blight and shoddy products. Government must impose its wisdom on the free process. It doesn't matter, said Nisbet, whether this thinking reflects disdain or concern for people. "Bureaucracy is a machine, and once present in mass and power, it has to be used."

Needless to say, these views are not universally shared. The threat to our form of government may be more from extreme inequality than from further equality, indicated James S. Duesenberry of Harvard. "Thus far we have been fortunate," said Duesenberry. "In our society, conflict over income distribution, and particularly between those with high income and those with low income, has been blunted. . . . We may find there will be more conflict in the future."

It does not seem likely that this conflict would be violent, although there have been revolutions in which small numbers of people have taken over governments. And whereas the race riots of the Sixties showed there *are* people in the United States who are intensely dissatisfied, revolution does not appear to be threatened because most people are dissatisfied with the form of government; there is not a majority demand for government to do more for the people. What bugs the average middle-income person is the manner in which the government role is being changed by taxation and income transfer. The danger to the republic does not lie in a revolt against poverty as it now exists or in a revolt against taxes. The danger lies in the massive dissatisfaction that would arise if the indirect economic effects of repressive taxation impoverished great masses of people.

Arthur Okun says the manner in which income is equalized is important. "I do not see a general trade-off between equality and liberty so long as equalization is pursued through the tax-transfer shuffle and other mechanisms that I recommended which do not include government control over employment or greater public ownership of the means of production." If these are the only choices, then taxation is certainly preferable to outright government ownership.

However, the distinction between the two choices is becoming blurred. If the government can take 70 percent of a man's earnings, the man is in effect working for the government.

Even on a theoretical basis, the right of private ownership is no longer entirely clear-cut. As has been noted, the phrase, "tax expenditure" is being used to describe the money left after taxes are paid. The inference is that people are given some chips to play with. The people then pretend they are playing their little game for money. When it's all over, the government takes back a portion of the chips, leaving the individual with a number that bears only a slight resemblance to the outcome of the game. In taking away chips, the government is reducing the individual's ability to exercise his freedom. Money is required to travel, to marry, to raise crops, and to buy books. If all income were taxed, there would be no effective liberty in these areas. If government collects more taxes this year than last year, there is less freedom this year.

The conflict between liberty and equality is admitted by some who favor greater equality. "We should, of course, restrict liberties as little as possible," said Marshall Cohen of the City University of New York. "But that liberty must sometimes be restricted cannot be denied." It can be argued that the subtraction of liberty from those taxed is balanced by the increased freedom of those on the receiving end. But in terms of the number of people affected, the balance is not even: there is a net subtraction from the upper three-fourths and a net addition to the lower fourth. Moreover, it is one thing for government to allow restrictive poverty to exist; it is another thing for government to intervene in a manner that restricts the freedom of the majority of people.

In both cases—at the receiving and at the giving ends—government is deciding how much money and how much effective liberty people shall have. This in itself is not a brand-new thing—there have always been taxes; what *is* new is the enormous size of the transfer and the formal assumption by the government of the right to determine how much equality shall exist. The propriety of this determination is defended by some on the grounds that concentrations of wealth in private hands frustrate the democratic process by giving undue power and influence to a few individuals. To remedy this condition by increasing government ownership and control means going from a relatively fragmented power structure to a truly concentrated structure.

As a practical matter, wealth doesn't seem to secure political privileges for the wealthy. The head of the United Steelworkers of America has far more political clout than the head of U. S. Steel: the steel companies tried for years to get government to curb imports, but not until the steel union and community leaders interested themselves in the question was there any action. Where wealthy people *do* become active in politics, they usually move in a liberal direction. That was true of Franklin Roosevelt, Nelson Rockefeller, the Kennedys, and others. All supported policies that were unfavorable to wealthy people. Rich conservatives tend to shy away from politics and public affairs. Business people are always being chided for failing to speak out on public issues. Apart from a natural inclination toward privacy, executives are conditioned by corporate traditions of caution and reticence.

Business is also inhibited by the knowledge that it can be punished by govenment in any number of ways. A few years ago, Kaiser Steel Corporation was charged with failing to meet environmental standards. Kaiser faced not only fines but the threat of government blacklisting. That would have barred Kaiser from government contracts; it would also have prohibited the use of Kaiser's products by customers on government work. The sheer size of government carries with it far-reaching power. The regulatory explosion has provided a ready-made instrument for directing, guiding, and restricting. This is seen as leading not to overt tyranny but to an enervating, nagging bureaucratic control. The process now at work in the U. S. can be identified more clearly in its advanced stages abroad.

Western-style socialism is described by Alan A. Walters of the University of London as the "slow, inexorable suffocation of our liberties by the bureaucracy under the heel of humanitarianism."

This may be an optimistic view. A pessimist would point out that most socialist countries are Communist dictatorships. Tyranny is overt and extreme.

Chapter 8

POLICIES AND SOLUTIONS

The growth of government has been partly a reflection of lack of growth in the private sector. This seems to run counter to much of what has been said in other chapters. Nevertheless, it is unquestionably true that some of the rise in government spending could have been avoided had the private economy been expanding more vigorously.

INFLATION AND GOVERNMENT GROWTH

From 1971 through 1978 there were three recessions and two years of sluggish recovery with high unemployment—in other words, five out of the eight years saw substandard economic activity. One consequence was that the government paid out $47 billion in unemployment compensation in the three years ending with 1977. There was a vast enlargement of public service programs—programs designed to take the unemployed off the streets and equip them with skills.

It can also be argued that the private lag was due to the government diversion of resources. That has been the long-term trend, and it is certainly true that taxation has held down

159

the economy. It is not true, however, that the manpower and machines for more vigorous growth were lacking; the problem has rather been underutilization. This has been because of a deliberate effort to repress the economy—an effort supported by those who would like to see greater government control of income—but the repression has been aimed primarily at fighting inflation. By holding down demand, we will keep prices from going up, supposedly.

Inflation is a very serious problem for all the obvious reasons: it all but strangles people on fixed incomes, it causes fear and unhappiness, and it provides a mechanism for overtaxation of both business and individuals. If prices were stable, the understatement of business depreciation would cease; people would not be hit with tax increases when there was no rise in real income.

One of the worst things about inflation, however, is that it is used to justify repression of the economy. When decisive tax cuts were proposed in 1978, there were dire warnings of inflationary effects. In 1969, the inflation fighters succeeded in causing a recession through tax increases and other measures. Repeated use of tax increases to hold down demand has contributed to the enlargement of government. In a reverse way, however, this has demonstrated that we now know how to regulate the economy. If tax increases will repress, it follows that tax reductions will stimulate.

This is a glorious discovery! One of the great failings of the American system has been its instability: there have always been recessions and depressions at regular intervals. This has been a very serious failing. If it is wrong to impoverish a man because he is lazy and incompetent, it is much worse to degrade an able, willing worker because the economy is in a state where there aren't enough jobs to go around. But we now know how to avoid recessions. It has been shown that the economy responds very quickly to the level of taxation. If the economy falters, it can be pumped up by cutting taxes: we can produce prosperity.

Unhappily, we are using our new knowledge to produce recessions rather than prosperity. This perversity stems from the belief that prosperity causes inflation, whereas recessions cure inflation. In periods of inflation, the recession cure is prescribed by both Democratic and Republican economists. "We know of no way of taming inflation and maintaining full employment," said Paul Samuelson, Nobel Prize-winning economist from MIT. "The rate of inflation will not come down so long as pressures of demand pushing on suppliers are strong enough so that higher prices and wages have no adverse effect on sales volume and employment," said Paul McCracken, who was chairman of President Nixon's Economic Council. In other words, the thing to do is have business so bad that competition will prevent price increases. This textbook remedy assumes prices go up because there is too much demand. That hasn't been the case with modern inflation.

THE WAGE PUSH

Prices have been going up in good years and bad. They have been going up because compensation has been rising about 10 percent a year. Under the best conditions, with a normal productivity gain, this rate would mean considerable inflation.

In recent years, the wage push has been compounded by lagging growth. When people are paid a lot more for producing a relatively small number of goods, the unit cost of production has to rise. The added cost pushes prices up. The magnitude of this push is indicated by the Westinghouse estimate that a man hired in 1978 will have a lifetime income

of $6 million if recent wage trends continue. At the end of
forty years, the man would be making $490,000 annually.
The system is elevating people's incomes, but it's too much to
expect that the average guy will really be making a half-
million a year within four decades. There has to be a lot of
inflation if wages and costs keep going up at the recent rate,
although it should be noted that the Westinghouse rate—8.55
percent a year—is not exceptional.

The implications of the wage push should be understood by
business. When you ask a businessman why his own prices are
going up, he'll tell you it's because costs are going up: there
isn't too much demand. But if you ask the same businessman
what's causing inflation, he'll say, in effect, it's caused by too
much demand: government spending results in budget deficits, and to finance the deficits, the government prints too
much money. Prices could not go up without a "fairly rapid
increase in the money supply," said H. L. Duncombe of

FIGURE 8-1. Compensation Increase Per Hour—Nonfarm
Business Sector

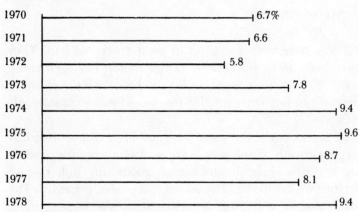

1970	6.7%
1971	6.6
1972	5.8
1973	7.8
1974	9.4
1975	9.6
1976	8.7
1977	8.1
1978	9.4

Source: Department of Labor, Bureau of Labor Statistics.

FIGURE 8-2. Unit Labor Costs Percent Increase—Nonfarm Business Sector

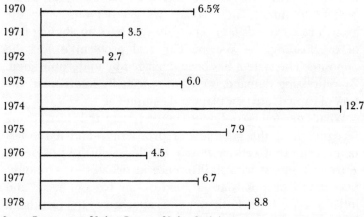

1970   6.5%
1971   3.5
1972   2.7
1973   6.0
1974   12.7
1975   7.9
1976   4.5
1977   6.7
1978   8.8

Source: Department of Labor, Bureau of Labor Statistics.

General Motors. "The market is validating these price increases."

It is no doubt true that the money supply could be manipulated in a way that would cause a severe depression and invalidate price increases. Someone has likened money to a string: it can be used to pull but not to push. You can say money policies have accommodated inflation by not pulling too hard, but you can't say the money supply has caused prices to go up; there haven't been too many dollars chasing too few goods. Nevertheless, we have been unable to get away from the automatic equating of inflation with too many dollars, too much demand, and too much prosperity. Accordingly, we have continued to fight inflation by holding down the economy.

Underlying this action is a lack of confidence in the system's ability to produce. Over the past forty years, the United States has fought three wars, rebuilt Japan and Europe, landed a man on the moon, and built enough TV sets for everyone. During World War II, we increased national output 50 percent in three years. Today, we get nervous when the growth rate exceeds 5 or 6 percent. We have an abiding fear of overloading the system. The real problem is just the opposite. The system has been damaged by underutilization. By repressing demand, we have repeatedly interrupted the flow of capital into new plant and equipment.

What's needed is confidence in the system and clear, strong recognition of the goodness of prosperity—and if the last point seems unnecessary, it isn't: the desirability of prosperity is treated almost with indifference in debates on economic policy. Tax proposals are argued on the basis of social and inflationary effects. Little weight is attached to the fact that a boom is much better than a bust.

Finally, we have to understand that recessions are not necessary evils in dealing with modern inflation; they are unnecessary, ineffective evils. Prices haven't been going up because of too much demand. They have been going up, as any businessman will tell you, because costs have been going up.

The big cost element in the average price is labor. According to Jerome Mark, assistant commissioner of the Bureau of Labor Statistics, labor costs comprise about two-thirds of the total cost increases faced by business each year. If labor's compensation is rising ten percent a year, prices have to go up. Attempting to suppress the price movement through a recession is not simply ineffective; it is the worst possible medicine. It compounds the problem by repressing productivity and thereby intensifying cost pressures.

The answer to the problem of inflation lies in finding some way to moderate the wage push. At the same time, there must be economic policies that promote progress and productivity.

THE 1975–77 RECESSION

From 1975 through 1977, the United States was in a recession. Unemployment ranged from 7 percent to 8.5 percent. There was about 20-percent idle capacity in most of this three-year period and as much as 30-percent in the worst of 1975. There clearly wasn't too much demand, yet consumer prices rose by an average of more than 6 percent a year. This experience did not discourage believers in the recession cure for inflation. By early 1978, with the unemployment rate around 6 percent, there were warnings against overstimulating the economy. One such warning came from Henry C. Wallich, a member of the Federal Reserve Board, who was quoted in the *New York Times* (May 31, 1978): "The net tax cut should be no more than $5 billion or $10 billion, not the $20 billion that the administration has now suggested."

Others began talking along these lines. In explaining how there could be too much demand when 6.1 million people were unemployed, the advocates of restraint came up with an ingenious answer: the jobless individuals didn't really exist. Most of them were unable or unwilling to work. In terms of qualified, available workers, 94-percent employment was close to maximum use of the labor force. The phrase "structural unemployment" was invented to cover those people too shiftless or stupid to work.

Although the incidence of subsidized loafing has probably increased in recent years, there have also been thousands of forced early retirements. In steel, aerospace, and elsewhere, highly qualified technical people have been fired outright. The euphemisms for this brutal process are "cutting off the fat" and "getting rid of the deadwood."

In the past, we have come close to full employment without inflation. In 1953 the jobless rate was under 3 percent, and consumer prices rose less than 1 percent. It's true many of the 6 percent unemployed in May of 1978 lacked skills, and the only way one becomes skilled is by working at a job: when there was a need in World War II, housewives became skilled welders and riveters overnight; schoolboys learned very quickly how to fly planes and steer battleships.

Apart from the matter of qualifications, the jobless problem is disposed of by questioning the accuracy of the government's figures. The unemployment rate is supposedly overstated by including those people out of work for short periods because of voluntary job changes. It's more likely unemployment is understated. Counted as employed in 1978 were many of the 3.3 million enrolled in public service programs. Not counted as unemployed were the 900,000 who had become discouraged and dropped out of the work force in early 1978. If those two groups were included, the unemployment rate in 1978 was over 10 percent. More than ten million people were unemployed, mainly because there weren't ten million unfilled jobs in the United States.

In August of 1978 plant utilization was around 85 percent of capacity. The justification of repression with 15 percent idle capacity was similar to that used in dismissing high unemployment. "The figures we see on capacity are slightly misleading," said William Miller, chairman of the Federal Reserve Board, "in that they talk in terms of physical capacity, not economic capacity. Many studies have shown we are nearly to the point now where using additonal existing capacity brings on high cost capacity, and this adds to inflationary pressures."

This is not a new theme. It pops up every time someone wants to justify unnecessary repression. The first time I heard about noneconomic capacity, I set out to document the fact that steel companies had a lot of facilities too old to be used again, but gave up the project when the treasurer of a major

TABLE 8-1.   Consumer Prices versus Unemployment Rates

YEAR	CONSUMER PRICE CHANGE	JOBLESS RATE CHANGE
1950	5.8%	5.3%
1951	5.9	3.3
1952	.9	3.0
1953	.6	2.9
1954	−.5	5.5
1955	.4	4.4
1956	2.9	4.1
1957	3.0	4.3
1958	1.1	6.8
1959	1.5	5.5
1960	1.5	5.5
1961	.7	6.7
1962	1.2	5.5
1963	1.6	5.7
1964	1.2	5.2
1965	1.9	4.5
1966	3.4	3.8
1967	3.0	3.8
1968	4.7	3.6
1969	6.1	3.5
1970	5.5	4.9
1971	3.4	5.9
1972	3.4	5.6
1973	8.8	4.9
1974	12.2	5.6
1975	7.0	8.5
1976	4.8	7.7
1977	6.8	7.0
1978	9.0	5.9

Source: Department of Labor, Bureau of Labor Statistics.

167

mill explained that the oldest furnaces could be operated profitably in a peak market. The rate of profit would decline, but the amount of profit would increase. The same point was covered in a 1978 interview of Lewis W. Foy, chairman of Bethlehem Steel Corp. "At very high levels of operation, marginal facilities, of course, are profitable," said Foy.

FIGURE 8-3. Capacity Utilization Rate in Manufacturing

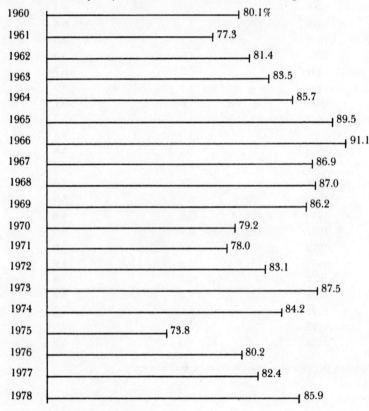

Source: Federal Reserve Board.

The trouble was, there weren't many high levels. For Bethlehem and other steel companies, 1977 was the third straight bad year. Bethlehem permanently closed major facilities at Lackawanna, New York, and Johnstown, Pennsylvania. "It's pretty difficult to sustain marginal facilities when you have cycles in the business, particularly when we were faced with very expensive environmental costs," said Foy.

In a cyclical industry, 100-percent modern capacity would not be desirable. The capital charges on unused new machines would kill a company in the slow years. It makes sense to keep a certain amount of older equipment for the occasional peaks. If the peaks never come, this equipment is eventually going to be junked. As this suggests, the warnings about noneconomic capacity tend to be self-fulfilling. If government decides there isn't enough capacity for full prosperity, then the capacity increment needed for full prosperity will disappear. The same is true of unemployment. If we decide a certain portion of the work force is unemployable, the individuals in question will eventually become unfit to work.

It shouldn't be necessary to argue these points. It is a fact that the economy was depressed from 1975 through 1977. In 1978 supply and demand were just approaching a comfortable balance. There wasn't too much demand for power plants or oil refineries or steel mills. Not enough was being done to increase the capacity and efficiency of basic industries. It was not true, either, that the capital lag reflected a diversion of excessive amounts into consumer spending. Private housing starts in 1977 were below the levels of 1971–73. Fewer new homes were built in 1976 than in 1963, a comparable recovery year. The recession of 1975 saw less homebuilding than the recession of 1959.

Sales of major consumer durables have risen at relatively slow rates since the start of the Seventies. The rise in government spending has been a general depressant rather than a selective stimulant. The failure of the slowdown to stabilize prices in the late Seventies did not deter those who felt recessions were the answer to inflation. The medicine was right, they contended; we simply didn't take a strong enough dose. The nation has not been willing to "bite this bullet," said Paul McCracken in August of 1978. In 1974, a similar diagnosis came from Milton Friedman. "Inflation is perfectly curable," said Friedman. By holding down government spending and the money supply, he indicated, prices could be stabilized. "But do we have the will to cure inflation? The answer is, in my opinion, that at the moment, we do not have the will."

The hard-liners are seldom explicit about the harshness of their cures. It is made to sound as though a few months without chocolates will calm things down. By 1978, however, some fairly harsh medicine had already been administered without success.

Charles L. Schultze, chairman of the Economic Council in 1978, called 1975 "the worst recession in 40 years. The rate of unemployment hit 9 percent. If someone wants to advise that, by God, you should get that up to 10 percent and stick with it for ten years and show your guts, the economics of that aren't very good." It isn't the economics that are wrong. There was no inflation during the ten-year Depression of the Thirties. If we're willing to accept another decade of shanties and breadlines, we could probably end the current price spiral.

Such a treatment is too awful to be considered. It is so awful it is impossible. "Quite apart from economics, it's not going to work," said Schultze. "This nation is not going to stand by and let a major recession occur."

THE PROBLEM OF LABOR COSTS

Fortunately, the causes of modern inflation don't have much to do with whether the economy is depressed or prosperous. Within limits, prices are determined by costs. This has to be true, because 95 percent of the average price is cost; the other variable, profit, is seldom much more than 5 percent. As has been mentioned, labor is the big cost item. Wages and salaries account for nearly 70 percent of the price dollar, and the influence of this 70 percent showed up very neatly from 1975 through 1977. Unit labor costs rose 18.5 percent in the three-year stretch. That almost exactly matched the 18.6-percent rise in consumer prices. This close alignment was not a fluke: from 1960 through 1977, unit labor costs rose at an annual rate of 4.2 percent; in the same period, the inflation rate was 4.1 percent as measured by the implicit price deflator and 4.4 percent as measured by the consumer index (consumer prices rose 4.1 percent a year from 1959 through 1977). In 1978, the 9 percent rise in consumer prices reflected an 8.8 percent rise in unit labor costs.

Apart from labor, other costs include property taxes, corporate income taxes, depreciation, and interest charges. Of these, only income taxes come down in a recession. This drop can be partly offset by the use of higher tax rates and higher interest rates to promote a recession. All the other nonlabor cost items are fixed. They don't change as volume rises and falls. This means cost per unit rises in a recession as fixed charges are applied to a smaller number of units, although some companies do gear depreciation to utilization.

The effect of low volume on unit fixed costs helps explain why the recession cure operates with reverse english. However, the most serious effect is on labor. Unit labor costs rise or fall according to pay increases and productivity gains. If

TABLE 8-2. Average Annual Rates of Growth—Private Business Sector, All Persons, Unit Labor Cost

	1961	1962	1963	1964	1965	1966	1967	1968	1969	1970	1971	1972	1973	1974	1975	1976	1977
1960	0.7	0.4	0.2	0.4	0.4	0.8	1.1	1.5	1.9	2.4	2.7	2.9	3.1	3.4	3.8	4.0	4.2
1961		0.0	-0.0	0.4	0.4	0.9	1.3	1.7	2.2	2.7	3.0	3.2	3.3	3.7	4.1	4.3	4.5
1962			-0.1	0.6	0.5	1.1	1.6	2.1	2.6	3.1	3.4	3.5	3.7	4.0	4.4	4.6	4.8
1963				1.3	0.7	1.5	2.1	2.5	3.1	3.6	3.8	3.9	4.0	4.4	4.7	5.0	5.1
1964					0.1	1.9	2.5	2.9	3.6	4.1	4.3	4.2	4.3	4.7	5.1	5.3	5.4
1965						3.7	3.5	3.7	4.3	4.8	4.8	4.6	4.6	5.0	5.4	5.6	5.7
1966							3.3	3.7	4.6	5.1	5.0	4.7	4.7	5.2	5.6	5.8	5.9
1967								4.1	5.3	5.8	5.4	4.9	4.8	5.4	5.8	6.0	6.1
1968									6.6	6.5	5.5	4.7	4.7	5.5	6.0	6.2	6.3
1969										6.4	4.8	4.0	4.3	5.5	6.2	6.4	6.4
1970											3.3	3.0	3.9	5.7	6.6	6.7	6.7
1971												2.7	4.4	7.0	7.6	7.4	7.3
1972													6.1	9.3	9.1	8.3	7.8
1973														12.5	10.1	8.3	7.6
1974															7.7	6.4	6.3
1975																5.0	5.7
1976																	6.5

1960	1961	1962	1963	1964	1965	1966	1967	1968
91.4	92.1	92.1	92.1	93.2	93.4	96.8	100.0	104.1
1969	1970	1971	1972	1973	1974	1975	1976	1977
111.0	118.1	121.9	125.2	132.9	149.5	161.0	169.2	180.1

To obtain the rate of annual change for any period, take the starting year from the column on the left and go across to the ending year shown in the top row. The bottom number in each column is the percent change for each year in the column.

The two rows of numbers across the bottom of the table are index figures for individual years.

Source: Department of Labor, Bureau of Labor Statistics.

172

TABLE 8-3. Average Annual Rates of Growth—Consumer Price Index

	1961	1962	1963	1964	1965	1966	1967	1968	1969	1970	1971	1972	1973	1974	1975	1976	1977
1960	1.1	1.1	1.2	1.2	1.3	1.5	1.7	1.9	2.2	2.6	2.8	3.0	3.2	3.5	3.9	4.1	4.4
1961		1.2	1.2	1.2	1.3	1.6	1.8	2.1	2.4	2.8	3.1	3.2	3.4	3.8	4.1	4.4	4.6
1962			1.2	1.2	1.4	1.7	2.0	2.3	2.7	3.1	3.4	3.5	3.7	4.0	4.4	4.7	4.9
1963				1.3	1.5	1.9	2.2	2.6	3.0	3.4	3.7	3.8	3.9	4.3	4.7	4.9	5.2
1964					1.7	2.3	2.5	2.9	3.4	3.8	4.0	4.1	4.2	4.6	5.0	5.2	5.4
1965						2.9	2.9	3.3	3.8	4.2	4.4	4.4	4.5	4.9	5.3	5.5	5.7
1966							2.8	3.5	4.1	4.6	4.7	4.6	4.7	5.1	5.6	5.8	6.0
1967								4.2	4.8	5.2	5.1	4.8	4.8	5.4	5.9	6.1	6.3
1968									5.4	5.7	5.3	4.8	4.9	5.5	6.1	6.3	6.5
1969										6.0	5.1	4.5	4.7	5.6	6.3	6.6	6.7
1970											4.3	3.8	4.5	5.9	6.7	6.9	7.0
1971												3.3	4.8	6.7	7.6	7.6	7.5
1972													6.2	8.6	9.0	8.4	8.0
1973														10.9	10.0	8.7	7.9
1974															9.1	7.4	7.0
1975																5.7	6.1
1976																	6.4

1960	1961	1962	1963	1964	1965	1966	1967	1968
88.6	89.6	90.6	91.7	92.9	94.5	97.2	100.0	104.2

1969	1970	1971	1972	1973	1974	1975	1976	1977
109.8	116.3	121.3	125.3	133.1	147.7	161.2	170.5	181.5

To obtain the rate of annual change for any period, take the starting year from the column on the left and go across to the ending year shown in the top row. The bottom number in each column is the percent change for each year in the column.

The two rows of numbers across the bottom of the table are index figures for individual years.

Source: Department of Labor, Bureau of Labor Statistics.

TABLE 8-4. Average Annual Rates of Growth—Private Business Sector, All Persons, Implicit Price Deflator[1]

	1961	1962	1963	1964	1965	1966	1967	1968	1969	1970	1971	1972	1973	1974	1975	1976	1977
1960	0.6	0.7	0.8	0.9	1.0	1.3	1.6	1.8	2.1	2.4	2.6	2.8	3.0	3.3	3.6	3.9	4.1
1961		0.9	0.9	1.0	1.2	1.5	1.8	2.1	2.4	2.6	2.9	3.0	3.2	3.5	3.9	4.1	4.4
1962			0.9	1.1	1.3	1.7	2.0	2.3	2.6	2.9	3.1	3.3	3.5	3.8	4.1	4.4	4.6
1963				1.4	1.5	2.0	2.3	2.6	2.9	3.2	3.4	3.5	3.7	4.0	4.4	4.7	4.9
1964					1.6	2.4	2.6	2.9	3.3	3.5	3.7	3.8	3.9	4.3	4.7	5.0	5.1
1965						3.2	3.0	3.3	3.6	3.8	4.0	4.0	4.2	4.5	5.0	5.2	5.4
1966							2.9	3.4	3.8	4.1	4.2	4.2	4.3	4.7	5.2	5.5	5.6
1967								3.9	4.3	4.4	4.5	4.3	4.5	4.9	5.5	5.8	5.9
1968									4.7	4.7	4.6	4.4	4.5	5.1	5.8	6.0	6.2
1969										4.7	4.5	4.2	4.5	5.3	6.1	6.3	6.4
1970											4.4	4.0	4.5	5.6	6.6	6.8	6.8
1971												3.6	4.7	6.3	7.4	7.4	7.2
1972													5.8	7.8	8.7	8.1	7.6
1973														9.8	9.9	8.5	7.6
1974															10.1	7.6	6.7
1975																5.1	5.4
1976																	5.7

1960	1961	1962	1963	1964	1965	1966	1967	1968
89.4	89.9	90.7	91.5	92.7	94.2	97.2	100.0	103.9

1969	1970	1971	1972	1973	1974	1975	1976	1977
108.8	113.9	118.9	123.1	130.2	143.0	157.4	165.4	174.8

To obtain the rate of annual change for any period, take the starting year from the column on the left and go across to the ending year shown in the top row. The bottom number in each column is the percent change for each year in the column.

The two rows of numbers across the bottom of the table are index figures for individual years.

[1]Current dollar GNP divided by constant dollar GNP.

compensation goes up 3 percent and productivity increases 3 percent, there is no rise in unit labor costs.

As has been mentioned, compensation has been going up about 10 percent a year in recent times. The historical productivity gain is around 3 percent a year. From 1965 through 1975, however, productivity advanced only 1.6 percent a year. There was a spurt in the 1976 recovery and a reasonable gain in 1977, but in the year ending with August of 1978, productivity rose only 0.7 percent.

Because productivity has lagged, a major portion of the labor cost increase has flowed into prices. The reason productivity has lagged is that growth has lagged. The slack that was supposed to cure inflation added to cost pressures.

In a recession, productivity suffers because people produce less. It's as simple as that. An individual company can improve productivity by reducing input—that is, by firing people. This is a one-shot thing, and it doesn't benefit the nation as a whole. National productivity doesn't improve when people are shifted from jobs to welfare roles. This was one of the problems in Great Britain. Plants were modernized, but an economic slowdown caused the added efficiency to reduce the number of workers rather than increase output.

For a real productivity gain, the nation must produce more. There must be growth. "That's the critical factor," said Jerome Mark of the Bureau of Labor Statistics. If there were no inflation, productivity would still be critical. Productivity is progress: it is what determines our living standard, and it establishes how fast real earnings can rise.

Because of the connection with real earnings, it is not accidental that compensation surged when productivity sagged. When there is little or no productivity gain, wage increases are eaten up by inflation. Unions feel they have been cheated. There are demands for catch-up increases the next time.

Taxation adds to the general unhappiness and to demands for more compensation. According to the Bureau of Labor Statistics, average hourly earnings rose 8.8 percent in the year ending July, 1978. With a 7.7 percent rise in consumer prices, the increase in real earnings was 1.0 percent. This small amount of progress was then wiped out by taxes. After these had been deducted, real spendable earnings were down 2.1 percent from a year earlier. As this brings out, taxes are part of the cost of living. To raise taxes in the interest of fighting inflation is completely contradictory. This contradiction helps explain why excessive pay increases don't necessarily create excessive demand. The full amount of the wage hike is paid out by the employer, and a major portion of this is passed on in prices. Because of taxation, the full amount of the increase is not converted into buying power. Incidentally, government spending in 1978 equalled 50 percent of disposable income for the first time.

PRICES AND PROFITS

As the 1978 statistics indicate, government's bite can be the difference between an increase and a decrease in spendable earnings. In a period of low productivity, this is almost certain to be the case. The effect of taxes on wage demands was discussed by Robert Bacon and Walter Eltis in their book, *Britain's Economic Problem: Too Few Producers;* in which they stated: "Deductions from pay packets grew so much from 1963 to 1975 that the average living standard . . . rose only 1.5 percent per annum—and since 1973 it has actually fallen." Demands for higher money wages led workers to turn to militant labor leaders. The point made by the authors is that workers won't accept a "social wage" in the form of government benefits in lieu of direct compensation; the benefits may be welcome but they are not equated with take-home pay. What makes all this important is that the profits are relatively unimportant. The profit slice of the sales dollar is a little over 5 percent in good markets and a little under 5 percent in poor markets (see figure 8–4).

Critics of the system stress the behavior of prices and profits in slow periods. In his book *Money: Whence It Came, Where It Went,* John Galbraith noted the ineffectiveness of the the recession cure and attributed this ineffectiveness to monopolistic tendencies. His opinion was that the market power of corporations and unions would keep prices going up as before. Galbraith didn't ask why corporate power wasn't exercised to a greater extent in good times. This is a key point. It is the absence of profiteering in strong markets that makes a profit squeeze so ineffective as an inflation remedy. In the 1973–74 boom, for example, profit margins didn't expand to 20 percent of the price dollar; they averaged 5.5 percent of sales. The 1975 slump brought a 19-percent reduction in margins, but the slice affected was too small to halt inflation; the consumer price index rose 7 percent.

That sequence was not unusual. Not since 1950 have profits accounted for more than 6 percent of the average price. There has been a healthy level of competition in good times. Intensifying competition through a recession does not correct a deficiency; it leads to destructive competition without having much effect on prices.

The charge that large corporations can price in an arbitrary manner was dealt with in a study by Steven Lustgarten *(Industry Concentration and Inflation* American Enterprise Institute 1975). Corporate size and industry concentration have tended to check inflation rather than promote it, Lustgarten concluded. "It appears that for the entire period 1954–73, the average rate of price increase for the high concentration groups has been substantially less than for the low concentra-

FIGURE 8-4. Manufacturing Profits as Percentage of Sales

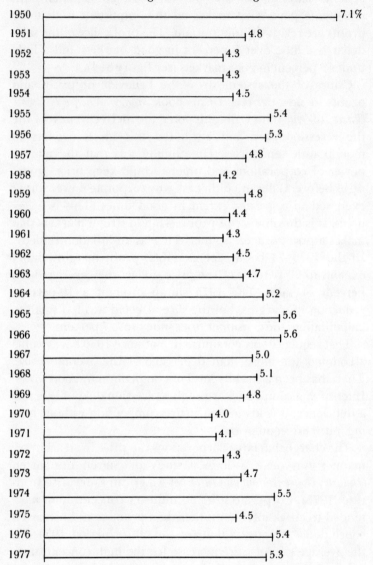

Year	Value
1950	7.1%
1951	4.8
1952	4.3
1953	4.3
1954	4.5
1955	5.4
1956	5.3
1957	4.8
1958	4.2
1959	4.8
1960	4.4
1961	4.3
1962	4.5
1963	4.7
1964	5.2
1965	5.6
1966	5.6
1967	5.0
1968	5.1
1969	4.8
1970	4.0
1971	4.1
1972	4.3
1973	4.7
1974	5.5
1975	4.5
1976	5.4
1977	5.3

Source: Federal Trade Commission.

tion groups." Part of the explanation for this pattern is that large corporations have the size and resources to use the most efficient technology. In basic industries, especially, the economies of scale make size essential. The Lustgarten study is one more proof that cost and efficiency are controlling factors in pricing.

From a market standpoint, corporate size does not insulate a seller from competition. Inland Steel Comapny has forced the much larger U.S. Steel to lower prices. Where size does come into play is in the buying of large corporations. General Motors can, and does, put tremendous pressure on suppliers. In the strongest markets, suppliers will think twice before raising prices of products used by GM. This helps explain why automotive sheet has been one of the least profitable steel products, even though demand for sheet is usually stronger than demand for other grades.

Throughout the system, competition is rarely, if ever, suppressed. We asked business people about this in 1971. "Our business is done in an auction market," said Douglas Jones, president of H. H. Robertson, a company that supplies industrial buildings. "Even in the strong construction market, we were experiencing declining margins." "How many companies have you seen that price themselves out of the market?" asked Semon Knudson, chairman, White Motor Company. "It will kill you." "We're selling a way of moving earth," said William Blackie, chairman of Caterpillar Tractor Company. "The contractor has an alternative. What we're selling is the least-cost way of doing things." "The market does regulate prices very effectively," said Alex G. McKenna, president, Kennametal, Inc.

You would not expect businessmen to say otherwise, but their statements are supported by the record. Profit margins have not increased very much in strong markets. "Profits don't increase prices," said William Blackie. When profits are good, he explained, business doesn't have to increase prices.

There are other factors at work. In the more conspicuous industries, prices are subject to varying degrees of government regulation. All pricing is probably more cost-oriented than in the days when Andrew Carnegie could cut wages and increase the workday. There is probably more of a tendency to boost prices in weak markets but also less of a tendency to take full advantage of strong markets. Ethical as well as commercial considerations have a restraining effect in strong markets. "The seller tried to protect his market from catastrophe," said Lewis Foy of Bethlehem Steel. "Certainly, prices would go up when there was a tremendous boom, but they would go up within reasonable bounds." He added that moderation was promoted by the knowledge that the market could change. "We have to live with these customers for a long time."

But, basically, it is competition that prevents profiteering. "Sellers don't set prices," said Foy. "Buyers do. The housewife determines what she pays in the grocery store. Someone charges too much and she stops buying. What happens? He cuts the price."

The constancy of profits is largely a reflection of the inability to profiteer in good times. It also reflects the ability of companies to make money in poor times. Profit margins of manufacturers have never dropped below 4 percent in the postwar period. This raises the questions: Why don't profits disappear in a recession? Why don't companies cut prices below cost?

The answer is that a great many companies do exactly that. More than 11,000 business failures occurred in the 1975 recession, and within large companies, individual operations failed. The steel industry shut down facilities rated for four million tons in 1975.

The change from healthy to destructive competition doesn't show up in prices, because costs have been rising so rapidly. The change doesn't halt inflation, because, again, competition is too healthy in good times to leave much room for squeezing profits. The point is, competition is not a fragile thing, to be snuffed out when demand rises a few notches.

THE KENNEDY DYNAMICS

The happy side of the wage-price equation showed up when the Kennedy administration took office in 1961. At that time, the Eisenhower administration's cure had left unemployment at 6.7 percent and plants operating below 77 percent of capacity.

The Kennedy administration set out to get things moving. In doing so, they provided a clear demonstration of the effectiveness of tax cuts in producing prosperity. Somewhat surprisingly, the first stimulants involved business taxes. These were cut in 1962 by installing the investment credit and by shortening depreciation terms. At the same time, the President's Economic Council enunciated a doctrine that called for wage increases to be limited by productivity gains. "The general guide for noninflationary wage behavior is that the rate of increase in wage rates in each industry be equal to the trend rate of overall productivity increase. General acceptance of this guide would maintain stability of labor cost per unit of output for the economy as a whole—though not, of course, for individual industries."

The guide for pricing was likewise related to productivity. Highly productive industries would cut prices. Less efficient industries would increase prices. The overall effect would be stability. All this was precisely what business had been saying for years. Nevertheless, the Kennedy program was received with distrust. Business leaders saw the guideline as a dodge for controlling prices without doing anything about wages.

The big shootout came in 1962 when the steel industry raised prices after the Kennedy administration had played some part in securing a moderate steel labor settlement. President Kennedy denounced the "steel barons" and eventually succeeded in rolling back the price increase. The episode left a bad taste, and the White House showed little enthusiasm afterward for intervening in wages or prices. The guideline policy degenerated into a government vendetta against the steel industry.

Business was really not too keen on the Kennedy tax cuts. There already was, and still is, suspicion of any government intervention in the economy. Tax reductions are sought as a matter of justice and logic. Any short-term tinkering is viewed with distaste. "An on-and-off stimulus brings some pretty bad long-term effects," said E. B. Speer, chairman of U. S. Steel in 1978. "It can't be a one-fix thing. We need long-term reform".

In 1962, the steel price confrontation made for extra unhappiness. "There is plenty of evidence the confidence of business in government is at a fairly low ebb," said Roger Blough, chairman of U. S. Steel in 1962. President Kennedy's comments on the subject of business confidence bear repeating: "I read that the problem really is that business confidence may be somewhat shaken by the action of certain public figures. Now, business had a high confidence in the previous administration, yet there was a recession in 1958 and a recession in 1960."

Despite the grousing by businessmen in 1962, the Kennedy program was enormously effective in stimulating business. For steel companies, the change in the depreciation rules added $114 million a year to depreciation charges. By 1965 the investment credit amounted to $90 million a year in steel.

There is a tendency now to lump together the 1962 reductions in business taxes and the 1964 reduction in personal income taxes when discussing the long expansion that followed them. Actually, the 1962 program had gotten things moving well before the second cut really took effect. Sales of manufacturers rose from $360 billion in 1962 to $443 billion in 1964, business capital spending went from $38 billion in 1962 to $47 billion in 1964, and unemployment fell from 6.7 percent in 1961 to 5.2 percent in 1964.

There was considerable debate in 1978 as to just why the Kennedy tax cuts were effective. Congressman Jack Kemp contended they stimulated supply. Walter Heller maintained they lifted demand. The lift provided by the earlier business cuts could be taken as support for Kemp's position. But, as he himself had said, demand creates supply, and supply creates demand. There was a further boost when income taxes were reduced in 1964. Throughout that year and well into 1965, national growth came primarily from the private activity. The Vietnam build-up began in the middle of 1965, but the 1965 defense budget of $49 billion was up less than $4 billion from 1960.

One of the most important things about the early Sixties was the absence of inflation. This was partly because wage increases were modest—about 4 percent a year from 1960 to 1965. Equally important, rapid growth produced a good productivity gain—about 20 percent from 1960 to 1965. As a result, consumer prices rose less than 2 percent a year. As this suggests, the rise in demand did *not* bring profiteering. Profit margins did rise—from 4.4 percent in 1960 to 5.6 percent in 1965—but this was largely the result of reduced costs.

THE JOHNSON-NIXON GAME PLAN

After 1965 there was a gradual reversal of economic policies. The growth strategy of the Kennedy administration gave way to repression. Attempts to influence wages and prices through government intervention were abandoned in favor of market-oriented regulation. All this may be mildly surprising, because many people trace the current inflation to the failure of President Johnson to apply the brakes when Vietnam spending escalated. The fact is, Johnson *did* apply the brakes. As has been stated, there had been only a modest increase in military outlays by 1965. There was a federal budget surplus that year.

When the spending bulge came in 1966, the Johnson administration increased business taxes by suspending the investment credit. The money supply was abruptly tightened. Federal spending did rise, but revenues went up almost as fast: the deficit was only $1.8 billion.

The restraints produced a mini-recession which ran through the second half of 1966 and the first half of 1967. In this period, which supposedly started all the inflation, wholesale prices were stationary for a full eighteen months. The economic pause had a predictable effect on productivity: efficiency gains fell from 3.7 percent in 1965 to 3.2 percent in 1966 and 2.3 percent in 1967. At this very crucial point, with the opportunities for real wage increases shrinking, the principle of wage guidelines was finally and officially abandoned. The February 1, 1968, Economic Report of the President said it was "unlikely" upcoming wage settlements would "fully conform to the trend in productivity."

Whether or not the government could have done anything to check the wage push is questionable. The guidelines had been pretty well repealed by the 1966 round of labor settlements. But if there was ever a time for trying to influence collective bargaining, it was in 1967. Instead, the Johnson administration looked the other way as a pattern of 6 and 7 percent increases was established in the auto, rubber, and trucking industries. In 1968 the Johnson administration gave

the economy a parting shot: a ten-percent income tax surcharge was applied, and this slowed things a little more.

By 1969 Richard Nixon was president. He gave top priority
to "the integrity and purchasing power of the dollar." The
Nixon game plan differed from the Johnson plan only in that
it was more explicit in its reliance on the recession cure and in
being even less timely. As measured by plant operating rates,
the gap between supply and demand had risen to 14 percent
by 1969. The steel industry, which was not noted for fierce
competitive instincts, had had an all-out price war in late
1968. In this setting, with no excess demand, demand was
repressed. Federal spending, which had been rising $20
billion a year, was held to a $9 billion increase in 1969.
Growth in the money supply was cut from 7 percent in 1968
to 1 percent by the second half of 1969. The investment credit
was eliminated.

These measures did slow things down. By the first quarter
of 1970, Gross National Product was falling at an annual rate
of 1 percent. Unemployment was up to 6 percent. The slump
had the designed effect of making it more difficult for
business to raise prices and maintain profit margins. The
profit portion of the price dollar fell from 5.1 percent in 1968
to 4.0 percent in 1970.

Prices rose because, in the absence of growth, there were
practically no productivity gains in 1969 or 1970. For the
whole economy, output per man-hour rose 1 percent over the
two years. In the nonfarm sector, there was literally no
increase. As a result, wage increases translated directly into
unit cost increases of 6.6 percent in 1969 and 6.4 percent in
1970. Profits were squeezed, but most of the cost bulge flowed
into prices.

The Nixon strategists did not ignore wages. The theory was
that the same market forces that produced price restraint
would bring wages under control. "As profits per unit

FIGURE 8-5. Growth, Productivity, Wages, Costs, and Prices

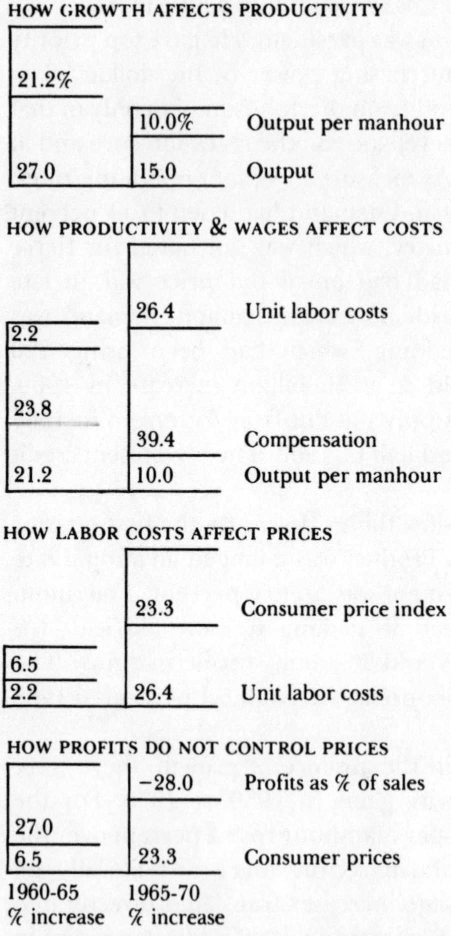

HOW GROWTH AFFECTS PRODUCTIVITY

21.2%		
	10.0%	Output per manhour
27.0	15.0	Output

HOW PRODUCTIVITY & WAGES AFFECT COSTS

	26.4	Unit labor costs
2.2		
23.8		
	39.4	Compensation
21.2	10.0	Output per manhour

HOW LABOR COSTS AFFECT PRICES

	23.3	Consumer price index
6.5		
2.2	26.4	Unit labor costs

HOW PROFITS DO NOT CONTROL PRICES

	−28.0	Profits as % of sales
27.0		
6.5	23.3	Consumer prices

1960-65	1965-70
% increase	% increase

Note: All figures except consumer prices and profits refer to the private business sector. Profits are for manufacturing corporations.

Source: Department of Labor, Bureau of Labor Statistics.

weakened," said the 1970 Economic Report of the President, "employers would become more resistant to granting wage increases. At the same time, a softening labor market would lessen workers' insistence on large wage increases."

This was a stunning miscalculation and one that has since been repeated. For management, the result was a case of overkill. The steel industry, which had taken a four-month strike in 1959, was in no condition to dig in its heels. "You're shut down and you're losing millions a day," said Stewart Cort, who was then chairman of Bethlehem Steel. Because of the profit squeeze, Cort noted, the industry didn't have millions to lose.

On the other side, the steelworkers had signed a 6 percent contract in 1968 and then watched prices go up more than 6 percent in 1969. You couldn't explain that in the absence of a productivity gain, there was no real progress available. To labor, it appeared that they had been bilked out of their wage hike. As a result, unions reacted to the slowdown with militance, not moderation. "Guess who's the fall guy?" demanded I. W. Abel, president, United Steelworkers of America (USWA). "Prices continue to escalate. Unemployment is on the rise," said Abel at his union's 1970 convention. He promised a "wage increase that will redress some of the economic wrongs we Steelworkers have suffered." Accordingly, the steelworkers demanded, and got, a 1971 settlement that raised compensation 10 percent a year. Other big unions did the same thing, and the nation was locked into an inflation rate of at least 7 percent.

There are two morals to the wage sequence. One is the tendency of a productivity lag to create a wage spiral. With real wage increases reduced, union demanded catch-up increases. The second lesson is that it is a mistake to expect unions to react according to the laws of economics. "A labor union is not just an economic unit; it is a political organization," said William Caples, president of Kenyon College, a labor negotiator for Inland Steel, and a member of the government's wage board in 1972. In politics, you don't survive by telling people they're doing fine and shouldn't always be asking for more. You certainly don't preach moderation when your constituents *aren't* doing fine—when they are being laid off and having their savings eroded by inflation.

It's possible, finally, that a labor cycle has a life of its own. Once the autoworkers settle for a certain amount, the steelworkers are going to demand at least as much. It's extremely difficult to end a wage spiral, because to do so means giving some union less than other unions have received.

One footnote to the Johnson-Nixon game plan: The initial effect of the 1968 tax surcharge was to increase government revenues and produce a budget surplus in 1969. In 1970, however, federal revenues fell by $5 billion; there were federal deficits of $12 billion in 1970 and $22 billion in 1971.

THE LESSONS OF THE 1960S AND 1970S

Looking back on the Sixties, two distinct patterns emerge (see table 8–5). In the first half of the decade, tax cuts promoted growth. The output of private business rose 27 percent from 1960 to 1965. This growth brought a good productivity gain of 21.2 percent. Compensation rose at a moderate rate of 23.8 percent. There was a negligible increase in unit labor costs and prices rose only 1.5 percent a year.

In the second half of the Sixties, everything moved in reverse. Tax increases repressed the economy. The growth rate was cut almost in half; there was only a 15 percent gain from 1965 to 1970. There was a comparable productivity slump; output per manhour rose only 10 percent from 1965 to 1970. Compensation increased more than 39 percent over the five years. Unit labor costs rose 26.4 percent and consumer prices went up 23 percent. Profit margins conformed to the reverse pattern. Margins increased when prices were stable in the first half of the decade; profit margins were shrinking in the second half.

The first portion of this object lesson was repeated in the Seventies when import quotas were established for footwear,

TABLE 8-5. Federal Spending and Receipts (in billions of dollars)

YEAR	EXPEND-ITURES	RECEIPTS	SURPLUS OR DEFICIT
1960	$ 93.1	$ 96.1	$ 3.0
1961	101.9	98.1	− 3.9
1962	110.4	106.2	− 4.2
1963	114.2	114.4	.3
1964	118.2	114.9	− 3.3
1965	123.8	124.3	.5
1966	143.6	141.6	− 1.8
1967	163.7	150.5	− 13.2
1968	180.6	174.7	− 5.8
1969	188.4	197.0	8.5
1970	204.2	192.1	− 12.1
1971	220.6	198.6	− 22.0
1972	244.7	227.5	− 17.3
1973	265.0	258.3	− 6.7
1974	299.3	288.6	− 10.7
1975	357.1	286.9	− 70.2
1976	386.3	332.3	− 54.0
1977	423.5	373.9	− 49.6
1978	448.6[1]	423.5[1]	− 25.2[1]

[1]Second quarter, annual rate.

Source: Department of Commerce; Office of Budget and Management.

color television sets, and specialty steels. The big argument against the trade restrictions was that they would be inflationary; protected from import competition, domestic producers would jack up prices in an arbitrary manner.

According to the Department of Labor, the actual effect was just the opposite. The affected products "have had smaller price increases than other comparable commodities and smaller price increases since import relief was granted than in previous years." The department indicated the added volume provided by reduced imports increased productivity in two ways. First, there was the direct, immediate effect of more efficient use of men and machines at higher production levels. Secondly, the added volume provided companies with the means and the incentive to modernize and expand.

For specialty steel companies, the combined impact was spectacular. "These productivity increases of 12 percent and 14 percent were higher than the increases for the economy as a whole (4 percent) and higher than the increases in the steel industry as a whole (1.5 percent)," the Department of Labor stated. Part of the productivity gain was translated into higher profits; that was why specialty companies had the money to modernize; but the big effect was on prices. In 1976, the year import quotas were applied, "wholesale prices of all stainless steel items fell in average by 4.6 percent. . . . One interesting facet, of the performance in specialty steel was that some of the quotas went unfilled during 1977," the Labor Department reported. In other words, increased demand did not weaken competition. It made domestic companies stronger competitors.

Similar patterns were noted for textiles, footwear, and color TV sets.

By the middle of 1971, President Nixon had had enough of the recession cure. He took the opportunity of an international dollar crisis to take the wraps off the economy and install wage-price controls. Business people were among those who applauded this action. "Heartiest congratulations on bold and timely moves to revitalize the American economy," wired Allison Maxwell, Jr., chairman of Wheeling-Pittsburgh Steel Corporation. "Clearly, in our industry as well as for the economy, the time had come for action," said James M. Roche, chairman of General Motors. "The day when we fight

FIGURE 8-6. Annual Rate of Change in Stainless Steel Prices and Wholesale Price Index for Materials for Durable Manufacturing

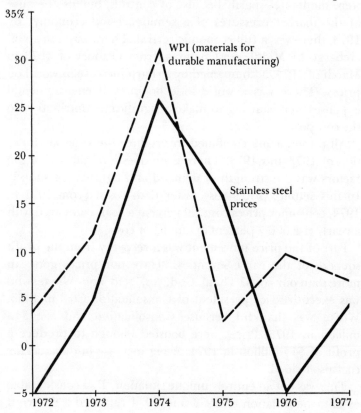

inflation with unemployment is over," said John Bunting, president, The First Pennsylvania Bank and Trust Company.

The wage-price regulation came August 14, 1971. That was just two weeks after the steel industry had signed labor contracts that would raise employment cost 10 percent a year. The steel contract was the last in a round that included workers in the auto, rubber, electrical, and trucking industries. From a wage standpoint, the Nixon administration was closing the barn door too late. The consequences of this timing did not show up in late 1971 or in 1972. Price increases were moderate—partly because of controls, but also because of the market pressures of a semidepressed economy. By 1973, there was a full economic revival. There was also an oil embargo by Middle East nations, from October of 1973 to March of 1974, accompanied by a sharp increase in world oil prices. There was a world-wide boom, and environmental expenses were starting to make a significant contribution to the cost push.

All these factors combined to produce the runaway inflation of 1973 and 1974. There is no question that one of the factors was the strength of demand and tightness of supply. In this setting, prices rose faster than costs. From 1971 to 1974, consumer prices rose 7.0 percent a year, compared with a yearly rise of 6.7 percent in unit labor costs.

Part of the price movement was a recovery from the profit squeeze of the early Seventies. "Have our prices gone up more than our costs? Thank God, yes," said Tom Whyte, who was executive vice president of Consolidation Coal in 1975. Whyte was thankful because Consolidation had lost $13 million in 1973. Prices were boosted enough to produce a profit of $43 million in 1974. A big increase in demand for coal also helped.

This was not an entirely unique situation. To a considerable extent, the inflation of 1973 and 1974 reflected a deferred cost push. Taking years of comparable prosperity, unit labor costs rose at an annual rate of 5.6 percent from 1968 to 1974, slightly more than the 5.5 percent rise in consumer prices.

It is still true that the inflation of 1973 and 1974 was intensified by the bidding for scarce products. Manufacturers were buying foreign steel at $100 a ton over the domestic mill price. Drivers were lining up at gas stations and eagerly paying premium prices. It is also true that when real demand inflation hit, two kinds of self-correcting actions took place. First, consumers stopped buying. "Auto demand in the fourth quarter of 1974 was in a state of collapse," said the 1975 Economic Report of the President. "Real consumer expenditures for energy . . . fell about 7 percent from 1973." Consumer resistance to high prices brought on a recession. A second correction in 1974 was in the field of expansion by industry. Oil companies stepped up domestic exploration programs. Steel companies announced plans for adding twenty million tons of new capacity. For industry as a whole, capital spending jumped more than $12 billion in 1974.

Supply does respond to demand, and to lack of demand: there was a steel shortage in 1974 because there had been no expansion of steel capacity since 1960; steel mills didn't expand because demand for their products was static. When there was market growth in the Fifties, steel companies increased capacity by fifty million tons. This was done almost entirely by rounding out existing plants. This is something that can be done in a relatively short time when there is a need. There are always bottlements in a manufacturing operation. Eliminating these produces a fairly quick expansion.

The point is, a shortage of supply will correct itself. Likewise, a shortage of demand brings a correction. People stop building new plants when old ones are only partly used. The earlier stops contributed to the 1974 shortages. When the Johnson-Nixon administrations suppressed demand, they also suppressed supply.

"We skipped a whole capital cycle," said R. J. Buckley, chairman of Allegheny Ludlum Industries, Inc.

There was another stop when demand receded in 1975. The steel industry scrapped most of its twenty-million-ton expansion program. There was a general pulling in of horns.

The pattern of the Sixties and early Seventies points, I think, toward a clear-cut solution to the oppressive problem of runaway inflation; it has been shown conclusively that high taxation is deadly for the economy, both directly and indirectly, and it has been shown that lower taxes stimulate the economy. The benefits and detriments to our way of life by government policy have been identified and substantiated.

Chapter 9

FUTURE DIRECTIONS

Periodic economic slowdowns were discussed in 1978 by Barry Bosworth, director of the Council on Wage and Price Stability. Productivity has been lagging, said Bosworth, partly because businessmen found it difficult to make decisions in an on-and-off economy.

As far as investment is concerned, there would be no difficulty if war were declared. Just before the Korean War, I worked for a company that was in the process of making a 10-percent reduction in the work force. When war broke out, the company began hiring people; without an order being placed, the fighting gave assurance of sustained, high demand. Economic policies should be able to provide something close to this assurance.

TAXATION AND SPENDING

As was emphasized in the preceding chapter, we do know how to produce prosperity and avoid recessions. It has been shown that tax cuts produce a positive economic response.

You'd think it would be a very simple matter to apply this knowledge. Everyone hates to pay taxes. "When the wage earner gets his paycheck and sees how much has been deducted for federal taxes, he is shocked and enraged," wrote Herb Stein. "He earned the money fair and square. It is his. And he doesn't want the government to take so much of it away from him. . . . In my opinion, it is a legitimate reaction."[1]

If an individual has a legitimate right to his earnings, taxes should be increased only with reluctance, and there should be a general disposition to reduce taxes. In *Money: Whence It Came, Where It Went,* economist John Galbraith says this slant does exist and that it makes for economic inflexibility. "If expenditures can be increased but cannot be reduced and taxes can be reduced but cannot be increased, fiscal policy becomes, obviously, a one-way street. It will work wonderfully well against deflation and depression, but not very well against inflation."[2]

Fiscal policy has not worked very well against the recent combination of inflation and depression, but the failure has not been due to an inability to raise taxes. It took Lyndon Johnson about ten minutes to increase business taxes by suspending the investment credit in 1966. By way of contrast, the income tax cut of 1964 was being considered in 1961, three years before it took effect.

The fact is, economic repression has both a liberal and a conservative constituency, although their thinking is widely dissimilar. Liberal thinking shows up in the myth that it is easy to cut taxes. Some years ago, Congressman William Moorhead (D. Pa.) suggested the president be given stand-by power to raise taxes. No such power was needed to cut taxes, Moorhead said, because legislators would rush to support proposals for reductions.

There was no rush in 1978. It took nearly a year to put

through a new tax bill. It isn't easy to cut taxes, but apparently it's easier than some liberals would like. The curious fact is that liberals have no enthusiasm for liberating people from tax burdens. The benevolence of the liberal movement runs toward government help and guidance. In the egalitarian writings, it is explicitly stated that general growth may have to be sacrificed in the interest of government-controlled sharing. It was this doctrine, said Irving Kristol, that Proposition 13 rejected. "In the end, there is the most important effect of all: a change in the climate of opinion affecting the issue of economic growth," said Kristol. The vote was against the idea that "Californians would be happier if only existing 'affluence' were more equally shared."[3]

Paradoxically, the case against tax cuts receives unwitting, indirect support from business. A 1978 paper of U. S. Steel outlined the business position. "Decisive tax cuts in individual and company taxes are needed, but it is imperative that government spending also be reduced." And since government spending isn't going to be reduced (spending has been cut in only 2 years since 1952), this comes close to saying taxes shouldn't be cut at all. It is true that spending can reach a point where tax cuts are impractical. It is also true that there have been budget deficits in times of high employment. But in a slack period, the sequence should be to cut taxes first and then try to bring spending under control.

Another business objection is that the use of taxes to influence the economy establishes a principle that can cut both ways. Companies have reason to be wary on this point, as the investment credit has been a convenient instrument for depressing and stimulating. In an imperfect world, however, business would be well advised to take what it can get and run.

Apart from self-interest, business people dislike any form of government meddling. Not fully appreciated is the basic difference between tax cuts and tax increases as economic regulators. A tax increase influences the economy by diminishing the private sector; it enlarges the size and power of the public sector. A tax cut does just the opposite; it liberates and enlarges the private sector, and it reduces the intrusion of government on the economy—in a sense, it regulates by de-regulating. Because the effects of tax increases and tax cuts are so different in character, endorsement of tax stimulants does not imply support for tax repression.

In any case, conservatives object to tax cuts because government spending is too great, whereas liberals object because the cuts will limit spending.

A little sidelight on taxation and spending is the terminology that has come into being: "Tax expenditures" are defined by the Congressional Budget Act of 1974 as "revenue losses attributable to provisions of the federal tax laws which allow a special exclusion, exemption, or deduction from gross income or which provide a special credit, a preferential rate of tax, or a deferral of tax liability." Joseph Pechman gives this explanation: "A tax expenditure, then, is a result of any deviation from the normal tax structure."

According to one authority, the phraseology was invented by Republicans as a means of showing that most tax losses resulted from commonplace deductions, used by the average person, rather than from the loopholes available to the rich. Said Pechman, "Including tax expenditures in the budget encourages the Administration and Congress to take them into account in budget decisions."[4]

Also encouraged is the belief that tax cuts are straight subtractions from tax revenues. No account is taken of the stimulative effect of a tax reduction. This very crucial point will be discussed later.

More important, the word "expenditure" implies that government has first claim on all income—The amount not taxed is spent, or given, by the government. *The Wall Street Journal*

(Oct. 31, 1978) had scathing words for the tax expenditure concept. "If you stretched this convoluted theory to its extreme, all the money the government lets anyone keep is a tax expenditure."

In the 1978 tax debate, all the theories and philosophies entered in. Had it not been for $180 billion in transfer payments, the federal government would not have been running a $25 billion deficit in the middle of 1978. Without the deficit, there would have been broader, stronger support for decisive tax reductions. Given the realities of the times, however, the 1978 debate hinged on judgments about inflation. Earlier, there had been signs of new thinking about the causes and cures of inflation.

"Clearly, the harsh 'discipline' of high unemployment and weak markets has done little to moderate wage and price advances in this period," wrote Walter Heller in 1977.[5] Conversely, the early Sixties showed there could be vigorous growth without inflation. "Just as inflationary salvation would not be found in running the economy way below par, so perdition does not lie in modestly stepping up the pace of expansion," said Heller. There were similar comments from Treasury Secretary Michael Blumenthal at a ministerial meeting of OECD in Paris, July 24, 1977. "Neither high unemployment nor low utilization of capacity leads automatically to a rapid drop in inflation. . . . So, we must now seek new programs and policies to supplement demand management." These remarks came in a session on economic growth.

THE 1978 DEBATE

In 1978, two events caused a change of tune. First, consumer prices rose at an annual rate of 9.5 percent in the first eight months of the year. Second, there was the 33-percent tax cut proposed by Congressman Jack Kemp and Senator William Roth. This combination brought a quick reverting to the old ways. The Kemp-Roth tax cut "would simply overwhelm our existing production capacity with a tidal wave of increased demand," said Walter Heller.[6] "Indeed, it would soon generate soaring deficits and roaring inflation," continued Heller, who engineered the Kennedy-Johnson tax cuts and who seemed oddly miffed that anyone should borrow his strategy.

His statement contained a strange mixture of contradictory viewpoints. He did not make the common mistake of evaluating the proposed tax cut on the basis of a completely frozen economy. The reduction would stimulate demand, he said. In no recent discussion has this important fact been questioned. Along with many others, however, Heller ignored the indirect effects of rising demand. He assumed tax revenues and supply would be relatively static. In predicting huge deficits, he appeared to take little note of how the wave of demand would increase tax revenues. In saying capacity would be overwhelmed, he seemed to assume nothing would happen to supply and capacity in an expanding economy.

The Kemp-Roth people pointed out that the whole picture was dynamic. A tax cut should "increase GNP, which is the tax base," said Jack Kemp, "and get back revenues to offset some or all of the initial cut." In support of this statement, he cited the effects of the Kennedy-Johnson tax reductions. Despite warnings by the Treasury of revenue losses, the next six years had seen a $54 billion rise in federal intake. Walter Heller objected that various factors were involved in the revenue rise, but the pattern of recent years is too clear to be denied and cannot be too often repeated: lowering tax rates has raised tax revenues; raising tax rates has lowered revenues. We have reached a critical point on the Laffer Curve.

Kemp also noted that prosperity would reduce the need for government social spending, and this obvious truth, as a keynote of this book, is a terribly important point. The manner in which a slowdown tends to enlarge government is brought out by a 1978 United Steelworkers of America statement on unemployment: "The most effective way for the government to help create jobs is through its direct job-creating efforts as embodied in the public service employment programs. . . . The possibilities in the public works area are endless."

A final point made by the Kemp-Roth people was that the tax cuts they proposed would do little more than offset tax increases due to larger Social Security deductions and the effects of inflation. A Congressional study indicated these would be adding $57 billion to the tax bill by 1981. The Kemp-Roth constituency rightly stressed the expansion of supply that flows from tax reductions. In arguing this point, however, they got into needless quibbling about the sequence of events According to the "supply economics" of Jack Kemp and others, the first effect of a tax reduction was to increase effort, saving, innovation, and risk-taking. These supply-related moves benefited the economy. This oversimplified the complex interaction of supply and demand and led to a great deal of scholarly wrangling. It is important to recognize that supply and demand move together, and it is reasonable to suppose that monetary incentives play an important role in this movement, but in setting economic policies, it is not necessary to get bogged down in a precise identification of causes and effects.

The fact is that from 1965 through 1978, the United States increased its productivity at about half the normal rate. This had to mean there were unused moral and physical reserves. If we would just turn the system loose, production would rise at a rate now considered impossible. All that's needed is to establish the principle that recessions are obsolete and prosperity is to be a permanent thing. In 1978, unforunately, it was not possible to get a strong consensus among either liberals or conservatives for prosperity. By a narrow margin, the Kemp-Roth bill was classed as too inflationary. Jack Kemp argued in vain that inflation wasn't caused by producing more goods. "I think Margaret Bush Wilson's statement is appropriate: 'Inflation has never been caused by too many people at work.'"

It is certainly true that one of the worst effects of the recent inflation would be dealt with in a vigorous, productive economy. Increasing the output of goods and services at a brisk clip would increase real income. Prices might go up, but incomes would go up faster. Inflation with full employment and rising real income would be a lot better than the recent combination of inflation with high unemployment and little real progress.

The ideal, of course, would be prosperity and full employment without inflation. And this is not an impossible goal: there was price stability and rapid growth in the first half of the Sixties, and there was little or no inflation in the Roaring Twenties. Sustained inflation in peacetime is a fairly new thing. In the first hundred or more years of the republic, there were wild price spurts during wars, but there was no long-term trend upward. Prices were lower at the end of the nineteenth century than at the start.

CURB INFLATION, OR PROMOTE GROWTH?

Part of the solution to the current problem lies in separating policies designed to promote growth from those designed to curb inflation. We should give full play to productive capacity and quit worrying about things being too good. Inflation should be treated separately—as a cost phenomenon. This perspective rules out remedies that add to costs. Increases in tax and interest rates fall in that class.

In dealing with labor costs, part of the solution would come as a free bonus. With sustained growth, productivity gains would offset reasonable pay increases. The trick is to get pay hikes down to reasonable levels. As long as wages go up 9 or 10 percent a year, prices are going to go up 6 or 7 percent a year. And as long as prices go up 6 or 7 percent, unions are going to demand 9- or 10-percent pay hikes. Labor unions hold the key to breaking out of the wage-price circle. By a process of elimination, this figures to be true. The one big change since the days of long-term price stability is the rise of organized labor. Companies were no less grasping and certainly no less monopolistic in the nineteenth century. Nevertheless, prices were stationary most of the time in those days.

The difference now is that pay patterns are set by unions that make demands, call strikes, and negotiate terms. This has changed the nature of inflation, because unions are insensitive to economic conditions. The pattern of 10-percent settlements was established during the recession of 1970–71. Most union contracts run for three years, so that no matter how bad business gets during the three years, there is no change in contract terms.

None of this is necessarily bad. The long prosperity after World War II was due in some measure to labor's insistence that workers be given a fair share of their output. The refusal of labor to reduce demands in slow periods has had a stabilizing effect on buying power and the economy. What is bad is that wage increases have spiraled to three times the rational level. Unions argue that wages are only following prices. That may be true, but it leads only to endless bickering over the assignment of blame. The fact is, inflation won't end while wages are going up three times faster than productivity. Prices will be stabilized if labor costs are stabilized.

THE BENEFITS OF A TAX REWARD

The way to halt the vicious circle is to have government take over a portion of the wage cost, which can be done by giving workers tax cuts in place of part of their wages. This would lower the costs of companies while preserving buying power. If this seems an outlandish idea, it is supported by a number of respectable authorities. Called a Tax-Based Incomes Policy (TIP), the new concept was endorsed by Henry Wallich of the Federal Reserve Board, Arthur Okun of Brookings Institution, and Lawrence Seidman of the Wharton School, who suggested that a 6-percent wage increase be the norm. For anything under that, employees would receive a tax break, whereas anything over it would draw a tax surcharge—and the same penalties and rewards would go to management *(Wall Street Journal*, March 30, 1978).

The idea of punishing management for "granting" excessive wage increases smacks of the Nixon Game Plan. The thought seems to be that big settlements are made either because management lacks spunk or because large corporations are in cahoots with large unions. The inference is that companies have a great deal of discretion in the matter. But if that were true, there would probably be no pay increases. As it is, settlements are forced on management by the refusal of unions to accept less. In 1978, which was an off-year for bargaining, the first nine months saw 45 million man-days lost in strikes. The last display of spunk came in 1978 when the coal industry took a 110-day strike. This didn't reduce demands one cent. The eventual settlement will raise mining labor costs 40 percent over three years. When a major industry does dig in its heels, the government will usually push for a settlement at any cost. Coal operators insisted they were bludgeoned into their settlement by the Carter administration.

Nevertheless, the idea of punishing overgenerous managements has been proposed in this country and has been applied in Great Britain. In a 1978 fiasco involving Ford Motor Company, the British government fined Ford for signing a king-sized contract. Nothing was done to the union which forced the settlement by striking.

Although it isn't likely that anything much would be done to offending workers in this country, the idea of a tax reward is both attractive and feasible. It's attractive because inflation won't be turned off overnight; if workers were persuaded to accept reasonable settlements and prices kept rising as before, there would be a disastrous shortage of buying power. As a practical matter, unions would not accept wage moderation without something in return.

THE CARTER INFLATION PROGRAM

The various TIP plans offer only a partial answer to the dislocations of the transition period. The tax inducement is a flat, one-shot thing. If the wage standard is 6 percent and a union settles for 5 percent, the difference would be made up by a tax cut.

That would be fine unless prices went up 9 or 10 percent. The Carter administration correctly determined that what was needed was not so much compensation for past inflation as protection against future inflation. Accordingly, the administration proposed a partial indexing of taxes. The wage guideline was set at 7 percent, and if prices go up more than that, there would be some kind of income tax reduction for the affected workers.

Having come up with a workable device for unwinding the spiral, the Carter administration weakened its program by not making effective use of the new mechanism. At 7 percent, the wage standard was set too high to start with; at best, it will produce a 4-percent inflation rate. The actual result will probably be higher, because there is bound to be some bending of the guideline. Shortly after it was announced, the administration made some concessions on fringe benefits. And it invariably turns out that compensation goes up more than estimates of contract costs.

Another problem is that the government's inflation protection is not in lieu of contract cost-of-living provisions. Contained in most major contracts, these provide that wages will automatically rise when the Consumer Price Index goes up a prescribed percentage. Where escalation is provided, the government's tax indexing is redundant. If prices go up more than 7 percent, wage increases will exceed the guideline. Nevertheless, Charles Schultze argued that cost-of-living contracts were preferable to contracts that anticipated inflation by providing large fixed increases.

That could be true. If the administration succeeds in winding down inflation, the cost-of-living provision will make wages follow prices. There would be an automatic moderating of the wage push. Without the cost-of-living payments, the current industrial contracts are not too unreasonable. The 1977 steel contract provided wage increases of 4 percent a year over three years. It is the cost-of-living payments that have been boosting the increases to 10 percent a year. Given the momentum of inflation, however, it is more likely that the cost-of-living provisions will continue to generate large payments. This is made still more likely by the fact that most contracts are front-end loaded. The 1978 coal contract calls for a 40-percent increase in compensation over three years with 20 percent of this to come in the first year.

There is one very practical difficulty with cost-of-living payments. Under the Carter inflation program, these were valued on the assumption that inflation would continue at 6 percent a year. If the steel formula is used, that means the cost-of-living provision will increase wages 6 percent a year. And that means union bargainers can have only 1 percent in negotiated wage hikes if they are to comply with the 7-percent standard. A union leader who came to his members with a 1-percent increase would not be well received.

It would have been better if the Carter administration had been bolder in its approach. A lower guideline with full inflation protection and no cost-of-living provisions would have been better. Nevertheless, the Carter program did address the source of inflation. It did so in an intelligent, imaginative way. The principle was sound; it just wasn't carried far enough. The real flaw in the Carter program was that it attempted to deal with two kinds of inflation. "First, we have to prevent the overheating of the economy," said Charles Schultze in December of 1978. "Second, we have to find ways to deal with the very strong inertia inherited—wages chasing prices, prices chasing wages."

To deal with overheating, the administration engineered a 1978 tax bill that left the average person paying higher taxes in 1979. At about the same time that the tax law was signed, the administration joined with the Federal Reserve in a series of highly repressive steps. The federal discount rate was raised to a record of 9.5 percent, and the reserve requirements of member banks were increased.

Administration officials denied they were promoting a recession. "In waging this war on inflation," said President Carter on September 20, "I reject the policies of the past. I will not fight inflation by throwing millions of Americans out of work. Such a policy is morally wrong." It was later acknowledged, however, that a partial braking action was intended. "We have set the dials to seek a lower but still reasonable growth rate," said Schultze. He added that the dials weren't precise enough to guarantee there wouldn't be a mild recession.

The trouble with all this was that the remedies for the two kinds of inflation were incompatible. Schultze noted that the inflation was primarily wage-price inertia ("I hate to call it cost push.") To the extent that the administration succeeded in slowing the economy, it would be aggravating the main source of inflation by repressing productivity. A 7-percent pay increase with little or no productivity gain would mean 7-percent worth of inflation. Unions would scream they had been betrayed. The wage guideline would be blown out of the water.

By the spring of 1979, it wasn't clear that any phase of the Carter plan would actually be implemented. The Administration was trying to persuade unions to abide by its wage guideline but legislation providing tax incentives had not been passed. The first big labor settlement—by the Teamsters—was somewhat above the guideline, and it wasn't clear Teamster locals would accept the terms. The rubber union was warning that it would pay no attention to the guideline in its negotiations. The economy as a whole did not recede in the first half of 1979. Capital spending remained high. The steel industry operated at maximum capacity in the first two quarters of the year. However, modest dips in auto sales and housing starts suggested a consumer recession might be in the offing. The first half of 1979 certainly did not see any easing of inflation. By the spring, consumer prices were rising at a double-digit rate. There were predictions that mandatory wage and price controls would soon be installed. There were calls for harsher repression of the economy.

By May of 1979, it wasn't clear how the Carter sequence would end. A reasonable guess was that there would eventually be a recession. This would partially repress inflation; the rate of price movement would fall to 6 or 7 percent a year. Capital spending would be cut. And then the cycle would start all over again. The basic problem will remain.

The problem is many sided and the same is true of the solution. The immediate need is to break out of the wage-price circle—to stabilize costs without crushing individuals or companies. This calls for extraordinary intervention by government. Tax reductions should be used to maintain corporate and individual income while providing the inducement for a moderation of wage and price increases.

For the long pull, we must recognize and utilize the capability of the American system of free, private enterprise. Given its head, the system will generate enough wealth to make everyone in the country wealthy. Given reasonable inputs, the competitive nature of the system will prevent inflation and force a downward distribution of wealth. This direct, private distribution in an exuberant economy offers the greatest hope for those who are now poor.

We now know how to keep the economy running in high gear. Reducing the tax burden of the private sector promotes growth and prosperity. We have not availed ourselves of this knowledge, partly because of inflation but also because of demands that government redistribute and equalize income. Redistribution can't do much more than raise people a few notches above the survival level. By subtracting resources and vitality from the private sector, redistribution is choking a system that could bring material well-being to everyone.

Notes

Chapter 1 THE PRIVATE SECTOR AND THE PUBLIC GOOD

1. Arthur Okun, "Equal Rights but Unequal Incomes," *New York Times Magazine*, July 4, 1976, p. 102.
2. Arthur Okun, *Equality and Efficiency: The Big Tradeoff* (Washington, D.C.: Brookings Institution, 1975), p. 68.
3. Colin D. Campbell, ed., *Income Redistribution: Proceedings of a Conference Held in Washington, May 1976* (Washington, D.C.: American Enterprise Institute for Public Policy Research, 1977), p. 214.
4. Irving Kristol, "The Meaning of Proposition 13," *Wall Street Journal*, June 28, 1978.
5. Okun, "Equal Rights but Unequal Incomes," p. 102.
6. Campbell, p. 106.
7. Edgar Browning, *Redistribution and the Welfare System*, (Washington, D.C.: American Enterprise Institute for Public Policy Research, 1975), p. 20.
8. Campbell, p. 181.
9. Ibid., p. 45.

Chapter 2 THE CREATION OF WEALTH

1. Colin D. Campbell, ed., *Income Redistribution: Proceedings of a Conference Held in Washington, May 1976* (Washington, D.C.: American Enterprise Institute for Public Policy Research, 1977), p. 36.

210

2. Helen Axel, ed., *A Guide to Consumer Markets 1977-1978* (New York: Conference Board, 1977), p. 198.
3. Robert Bacon and Walter Eltis, *Britain's Economic Problem: Too Few Producers* (New York: St. Martin's Press, 1978).
4. Conference Board, *Across the Board*, October 1977.
5. Ibid.

Chapter 7 GOVERNMENT SOCIAL SPENDING

1. George F. Break and Joseph A. Pechman, *Federal Tax Reform: The Impossible Dream?* (Washington, D.C.: Brookings Institution, 1975).
2. Arthur Okun, *Equality and Efficiency: The Big Tradeoff* (Washington, D.C.: The Brookings Institution, 1975), p. 68.
3. Edgar K. Browning, *Redistribution and the Welfare System* (Washington, D.C.: American Enterprise Institute for Public Policy Research, 1975), p. 118.
4. Colin D. Campbell, ed., Income Redistribution: Proceedings of a Conference Held in Washington, May 1976 (Washington, D.C.: American Enterprise Institute for Public Policy Research, 1977).
5. *New York Times,* August 8, 1976.
6. Okun, p. 103.
7. Browning, p. 102-3.
8. Milton Friedman, "Tax Reform: An Impossible Dream," Newsweek, April 12, 1976.
9. Campbell, p. 215.

Chapter 9 FUTURE DIRECTIONS

1. Herbert Stein, "The Real Reason for a Tax Cut," *Wall Street Journal,* July 18, 1978.
2. John K. Galbraith, *Money: Whence It Came, Where It Went* (Boston: Houghton Mifflin, 1975), p. 184.
3. Irving Kristol, "The Meaning of Proposition 13," *Wall Street Journal,* June 28, 1978.
4. Joseph A. Pechman, ed., *Setting National Priorities–The 1979 Budget* (Washington, D.C.: Brookings Institution, 1978), p. 315.
5. Walter W. Heller, "The Battle Against Inflation," *Wall Street Journal,* April 6, 1977.
6. Walter W. Heller, "The Kemp-Roth-Laffer Free Lunch," *Wall Street Journal,* July 12, 1978.

Index

Index

Index